Anonymus

Return of judicial statistics of Ireland, 1898

Part II: Civil proceedings in central and district courts

Anonymus

Return of judicial statistics of Ireland, 1898
Part II: Civil proceedings in central and district courts

ISBN/EAN: 9783742812698

Manufactured in Europe, USA, Canada, Australia, Japa

Cover: Foto ©Lupo / pixelio.de

Manufactured and distributed by brebook publishing software
(www.brebook.com)

Anonymus

Return of judicial statistics of Ireland, 1898

JUDICIAL STATISTICS, IRELAND, 1898.

PART II.—CIVIL STATISTICS.

STATISTICS RELATING TO CIVIL PROCEEDINGS

IN

Supreme Courts of Appeal; the Divisions of the High Court of Justice; the Court of the Irish Land Commission; and in Larger and Smaller District Courts—Law Stamps and Taxes—Consolidated Taxing Offices—Registration of Judgments, Titles, Deeds, &c., for the Year 1898.

Presented to both Houses of Parliament by Command of Her Majesty.

DUBLIN:

PRINTED FOR HER MAJESTY'S STATIONERY OFFICE,

BY ALEXANDER THOM & CO. (LIMITED).

And to be purchased, either directly or through any Bookseller, from
Hodges, Figgis, and Co. (Limited), 104, Grafton-street, Dublin; or
Eyre and Spottiswoode, East Harding-street, Fleet-street, E.C., and
32, Abingdon-street, Westminster, S.W.; or
John Menzies and Co., 12, Hanover-street, Edinburgh, and 90, West Nile-street, Glasgow.

1900.

[C. 9494.] *Price 9d.*

Charlemont House, Dublin,

28th *April*, 1900.

Sir,

I have the honour to submit herewith, for the consideration of His Excellency the Lord Lieutenant, Part II. of the Judicial Statistics of Ireland for the year 1899, consisting of my Report on the Civil Statistics for the year, with appended Tables

I remain, Sir,

Your obedient servant,

ROBERT E. MATHESON,

Registrar-General.

The Under Secretary,

&c., &c., &c.,

Dublin Castle.

CONTENTS OF REPORT.

CONTENTS OF APPENDIX OF TABLES.

I. CENTRAL ADMINISTRATION OF JUSTICE.

High Court of Justice.

Table

Law Taxes—

Appellate Jurisdiction—

II. LOCAL ADMINISTRATION OF JUSTICE.

Larger Districts.

County Courts—

Irish Land Commission—

Sheriffs' Proceedings—

Jurors—

Quarter Sessions—

III. LOCAL ADMINISTRATION OF JUSTICE.

Smaller Districts.

INDEX TO SUBJECTS

IN

REPORT AND TABLES.

c 2

JUDICIAL STATISTICS OF IRELAND

FOR THE

YEAR 1898.

PART II.—CIVIL STATISTICS.

The Tables in this part include Statistics relating to the Civil Jurisdiction of all Courts in Ireland.

The Courts and Offices are divided into those which relate to the Central Administration of Justice, and those connected with the Local Administration of Justice, the latter being classified into larger and smaller District Administration of Justice, according to the nature and extent of the Special Jurisdiction. *Arrangement of Tables.*

I.—CENTRAL ADMINISTRATION OF JUSTICE.

The Central Administration of Justice includes the High Court of Justice, consisting of two divisions—Chancery and Queen's Bench—and the Court of the Land Commission. Under the head of the Queen's Bench are now included the former Queen's Bench, Exchequer, Common Pleas, and Probate and Matrimonial Divisions, the High Court of Admiralty, and the Court of Bankruptcy. *Central Administration of Justice.*

The Central Appellate Jurisdictions, viz., Her Majesty's Court of Appeal, Ireland; Court for Cases Reserved for Judges of the Queen's Bench Division; the Privy Council in Ireland; Her Majesty in Council; and the House of Lords; have been grouped along with the other Central Jurisdictions, as they are closely connected with them. The proceedings in the Court for Crown Cases Reserved are dealt with in Part I., Criminal Statistics.

Central Administration of Justice.

Chancery Division.

Business in Court before Lord Chancellor, Master of the Rolls, and Vice-Chancellor. Tables I. 2.

HIGH COURT OF JUSTICE—CHANCERY DIVISION.

The following summary shows the Court business in the Chancery Division during the years 1897 and 1898, with the increase or decrease under each head in the latter year :—

COURT BUSINESS IN CHANCERY DIVISION.	1897.	1898.	Increase, 1898.	Decrease, 1898.
BEFORE LORD CHANCELLOR.				
(N.B.—The Lord Chancellor sits constantly as President of the Court of Appeal during five days of the week. He also exercises under the Queen's Sign Manual, the sole jurisdiction in Lunacy. For his Orders, made in that Department, see p. 18 *infra.*)				
Orders on motions special or from Chambers,	33	29	–	4
Orders on motions of course,	–	–	–	–
Orders on petitions of course,	–	4	4	–
Orders on petitions heard,	6	–	–	6
Actions, &c., heard,	–	–	–	–
Motions for judgment heard,	1	–	–	1
Causes, actions, &c., for further consideration heard,	–	–	–	–
	40	33	–	7
BEFORE MASTER OF THE ROLLS.				
Orders on motions special or from Chambers,	334	326	–	8
Orders on motions of course,	143	247	104	–
Orders on petitions heard,	19	9	–	10
Actions, &c., heard,	38	48	10	–
Motions for judgment heard,	33	29	4	–
Causes, actions, &c., for further consideration heard,	36	18	–	14
	514	682	161	–
BEFORE VICE-CHANCELLOR.				
Orders on motions special or from Chambers,	136	134	–	11
Orders on motions of course,	133	243	110	–
Orders on petitions of course,	2	8	6	–
Orders on petitions heard,	16	11	–	5
Orders on County Court Appeals,	8	7	–	3
Actions, &c., heard,	38	40	2	–
Motions for judgment heard,	24	28	4	–
Causes, actions, &c., for further consideration heard,	16	14	–	3
County Court equity appeals heard, *	3	1	–	2
	431	533	102	–
Total,	980	1,224	246	–

This table shows an increase of Court business of 240 proceedings, following a decrease of 75 in 1897.

Registrars' Office. Table I.

In the office of the Registrars of the Chancery Division, the total number of Side Bar Orders was 62, or 19 under the number for 1897.

* There were also three such Appeals before the Lord Judges in 1897 and one in 1898.

From the County Court equitable jurisdiction, up to £500 property and £30 a year in land, 2 Appeals were argued during the year: both were dismissed with costs. Three appeals were pending at the end of the year.

Central Administration of Justice.

Chancery Division.

The following is a summary of the principal proceedings in the Chambers of the Lord Chancellor, the Master of the Rolls, and the Vice-Chancellor:—

Chief Clerks Returns of proceedings in Chambers. Table 3.

Proceedings in Chambers of Chancery Judges.	1898.	1897.	Increase, 1898.	Decrease, 1898.
Summonses:—				
To make Infants Wards,	30	37	-	9
For the Administration of Estates,	160	167	-	15
Under the Charitable Trusts Act,	-	-	-	-
For appointment of Guardians and maintenance of Infants / For other purposes,	303	353	-	50
Other Summonses than to originate Proceedings,	1,079	1,060	19	-
Appointments (by Summonses, &c.), disposed of,	3,839	3,973	-	134
Orders made*:—				
Of the Class drawn up by the Registrars,	260	275	-	57
Of the Class drawn up in Chambers,	1,087	1,071	16	-
Orders brought into Chamber for prosecution:—				
Other than Orders for winding up Companies,	673	393	-	17
For winding up Companies,	5	6	1	-
Number of Advertisements issued,	192	183	-	9
Receivers' and Trustees' Accounts passed,	50	53	0	-
Receipts therein,	£194,325	£141,773	-	£53,554
Disbursements and Allowances therein,	£182,444	£138,850	-	£45,594
Accounts passed other than Receivers' Accounts:—				
Number of Accounts,	228	189	-	41
Receipts therein,	£[illegible]	£[illegible]	-	£108,709
Disbursements and allowances therein,	£284,[illegible]	£485,[illegible]	-	£118,781

The amount of property passed in accounts fell from £863,391 in 1897 to £704,124, being a decrease of £158,267, following a decrease of £160,246 in 1897 as compared with 1896.

In the Lord Chancellor's, the Master of the Rolls', and the Vice-Chancellor's Chambers there were at the end of the year 750 Wards of Court. The new Minor or Infancy Matters in the year were 23, relating to 55 Wards, as compared with 31 new Matters and 60 new Wards in 1897.

Minor matters in Chambers.

The number of actions by writ of summons was 807, showing an increase of 290 as compared with the number (517) in 1897, which was 30 over that for 1896. The proportion of lower scale to higher scale was as 47 to 53 per cent. The originating summonses (440) are 19 more than the summonses filed (421) in 1897. In the Notice Department there were 19,724 original documents, being 2,180 over the number in 1897, which was 849 under that for 1896; and 47,527 copies, being 9,678 over the number in 1897, which was 1,471 under that for 1896.

Clerk of Records and Writs. Table 4.

The Lord Chancellor made 81 orders on Petitions as to Commissioners for administering oaths for the High Court of Justice. There were 6 orders on Petitions

Lord Chancellor's Secretary. Table 5.

* Since the 15th April, 1878, all Orders made on originating summonses, as well as all Orders made on summonses in any suit prior to decree, and all like Orders dealing with separate estates have been made by the Registrars, and not by the Chief Clerk, as heretofore.

General Administration of Justice. — *Chancery Division.*

as to Notaries. The orders as to other Petitions, including Minor Matters, were 19. The warrants for Magistrates were 151, as compared with 177 in 1897, and 238 in 1896. There were no warrants as to Coroners.

Secretary at the Rolls. Table 5.

The return of the Secretary at the Rolls included in Table 5 gives the particulars of the petitions set down for hearing before the Master of the Rolls.

Crown and Hanaper Office. Table 4.

The number of proceedings in the Crown and Hanaper Office was 2,429, being 513 over the number during the year 1897, which showed a decline of 557 as compared with the number of proceedings in 1896.

Land Judge.

Land Judge Registrar's Returns. Table 6.

Under the Land Judge the net rental or annual value (where given) of Estates sold in the year ended 1st November, 1898, was £24,583, as compared with £18,009 in 1897, £33,016 in 1896, £22,079 in 1895, £29,052 in 1894, £23,615 in 1893, £38,986 in 1892, £28,623 in 1891, and £15,896 in 1890, and the purchase-money was £894,358, as compared with £272,177 in 1897, £517,403 in 1896, £356,371 in 1895, £447,999 in 1894, £393,165 in 1893, £500,860 in 1892, £410,491 in 1891, and £249,413 in 1890. As the properties sold did not consist solely of fee-simple lands, the several amounts here set forth include the purchase-money of life estates and other limited terms as well as of lands in fee.

The number of cases pending at the end of the year in the Judge's Chamber was 2,629, as compared with 2,838 in 1897, and 2,904 in 1896.

Record and Affidavit Office. Table 7.

The number of petitions filed in the year ended 31st October, 1898, was 69, being 8 under the number in the preceding year, and 14 under that for 1896, only 13 being by owners. The number of affidavits filed, 2,028, is 181 under that for 1897, but 79 over the number for 1896.

Receipt of Deeds. Table 8.

The number of abstracts of title lodged was 52, and the number of deeds and other documents lodged 2,896; in 1897 the respective corresponding numbers were 57 and 2,574.

Queen's Bench Division.*

Business in Queen's Bench Division. Tables 10, 11, 12, and 14.

The proceedings at the Plea side of the Queen's Bench Division* are arranged in a single table, although the figures have been supplied by three officers—the Clerk of Writs, the Master, and the Registrar.

Writs of summons, which had risen from 16,754 in 1896 to 20,166 in 1897, fell to 19,986 in 1898. The number of cases which actually came to trial by jury in Dublin in 1898 was 815, being 77 over the number in 1897, and 105 over that for 1896; the amount of money recovered at these trials, which had risen from £12,096 in 1896 to £16,039 in the following year, fell to £14,410 in 1898. In this connection it may be observed that the amount and importance of Judicial business in Ireland, where there is so much litigation respecting title to land and to easements, cannot be at all adequately estimated from the mere amounts either claimed or recovered by suitors.

Of the other business of the Division on the Plea side, there were 19,324 affidavits, an increase of 1,015, as compared with the number in 1897.

* The Exchequer Division was, by the Supreme Court of Judicature Act, 1897, amalgamated with the Queen's Bench Division on 5th August, 1897.

Central Administration of Justice.

Queen's Bench Division.

Business in Queen's Bench Division. Tables 10, 11, 12, 13, and 14.

The return of the business at Chambers and before a single Judge in Court shows that the number of summonses in 1898 was 295 or 12 under the number in 1897; that the number of motions on notice before a single Judge was 540 or 837 under that for the preceding year; and that the exparte motions (including consent orders) granted, were 1,594 or 38 under the number in 1897.

Appeals heard before Judges of Consolidated Jury Trial Court. Table 15.

The Judges for Jury trials in Dublin also hear Appeals from the Courts of the Recorder, the County Court Judge for the City and County of Dublin.

The statistics of these appeals or rehearings in 1897 and 1898 are as follows:—

Appeals (Rehearings).		Entered.	Affirmed.	Reversed.	Remitted, Struck out, &c.	Remaining.
From Decrees or Dismiss of Recorder of Dublin City and County Courts (including cases stated),	1897,	87	63	18	11	–
	1898,	98	60	17	18	3

Cases remitted to County Courts. Table 16.

The proceedings as to applications to have cases remitted to County Courts are as follows:—

Proceedings under Stat. [illegible] Vic., cap. [illegible].	1897.	1898.	Increase, 1898.	Decrease, 1898.
Number of applications to remit to inferior Courts,	411	396	–	18
Number of applications refused,	69	35	–	34
Number of applications granted,	343	361	18	–
In Cases of Contract under £50.				
Number of applications granted,	169	178	9	–
In Cases of Tort.				
Number of applications granted under sec. 6,	176	183	–	33

It appears from this table that the number of applications to remit cases to the County Courts was 396, showing a decrease of 16 as compared with the year 1897, the number for which year was 27 over that for 1896. Of the 861 applications granted, 178 were in cases of contract and 183 in cases of tort.

The civil business of the Judges of the High Court on Circuit is dealt with at page 21.

Proceedings at the Crown side. Table 17.

The Queen's Coroner, Attorney and Master of the Crown Office has made his usual return of the business at the Crown side of the Queen's Bench. See Table 17.

Election Petitions. Table 18.

There were no election petitions in 1898.

Acknowledgments by Married Women. Table 19.

No acknowledgments by married women were filed during the year 1898; one such acknowledgment was filed in 1897. Under the provisions of the Conveyancing Act, 1882 (45 & 46 Vic., cap. 39, sec. 7), no Certificates and Affidavits of Acknowledgment are filed, save such as relate to Deeds executed before the commencement of the Act.

No Perpetual Commissioners were appointed during either 1897 or 1898; in the year 1896, 8 appointments were made. The number of Special Commissions granted during 1898 was 5, being 2 more than in 1897.

Central Administration of Justice. — *Queen's Bench Division.* — Revenue Side. Tables 11 and 20. Registry of Judgments Office. Table 21.

The writs issued on the Revenue side in 1898 were 401, and the affidavits filed 59; there was only one Side Bar Rule.

OFFICES OF REGISTRATION.

The number of judgments, &c., registered in the Registry of Judgments Office in 1898, as compared with the preceding year, was as follows:—

Registry of Judgments Office.	1897.	1898.	Increase, 1898.	Decrease, 1898.
Judgments of Superior Courts registered,	2,729	2,901	172	–
" " re-registered,	130	94	–	36
Revivals,	–	–	–	–
Decrees, Rules, and Orders,	–	–	–	–
Lis pendens, registered,	1,087	650	–	437
" re-registered,	53	49	–	4
Judgments from Courts in England and Scotland registered,	20	19	–	1
Total,	4,019	3,713	–	306
Recognizances registered,	134	107	–	27
" re-registered,	36	80	44	–
Crown Bonds registered,	99	110	11	–
" re-registered.	42	80	38	–
Total,	311	377	66	–
Satisfactions of Judgments,	81	73	–	8
Vacates of Recognizances, and Cancellations of Crown Bonds.	166	90	–	76
Negative Searches on £1 Stamps,	1	–	–	1
" " 1s. Stamps,	2,157	2,213	56	–
" " 2s. 6d. Stamps,	52	18	–	34
Total,	2,457	2,393	–	64
Requisitions for liberty to search made by public,	8,194	7,530	–	664
Stamped Certificates issued,	5,722	4,878	–	844

The figures in the above table show on the whole, a decrease of business in the office in 1898, as compared with 1897, in which year the volume of business was greater than in 1896. The number of Judgments of the Irish Superior Courts registered was 2,901, being 172 over the number for the year 1897, and 585 over that for 1896.

In the latter part of 1898 the compulsory registration of Recognizances, as a charge against Real Estate was dispensed with, unless specially ordered.

None of the Irish Judgments registered in 1898 were obtained before 15th July, 1850 (which judgments alone affect land without being registered in the Deeds Office as a Judgment Mortgage): of the 94 Judgments re-registered, 92 were obtained before 15th July, 1850, and 2 since that date.

On comparing the number of judgments registered with the number of executions issued on Judgments in the Queen's Bench Division, it appears that 6,170 judgment executions are returned in the proceedings in Master's Office as entered up, and that 2,901 judgments were registered in the Registry of Judgments Office. General Administration of Justice.

Table 23 contains a return of proceedings in the Local Registration of Title (Ireland) Office, under 54 and 55 Vic., cap. 66, for the year 1898. During the year there were 476—464 compulsory, and 12 voluntary—applications to register in cases completed by the Land Commission before the end of 1891 (in which a written application and examination of the Title are required): the Titles in 471 of these cases were read, and 893 Searches issued. The total number of current cases (*i.e.*, cases sent down from day to day by the Land Commission, and registered as of course, no application being necessary), and application cases registered during the year was 5,045. In the two years, 1892 and 1893, which were the first years during which the Act of 1891 was in operation, 6,627 cases were registered; in the year 1894 there were 3,882 cases registered; in the following year the cases registered numbered 4,184; in 1896 the number was 3,899; and in 1897 it was 3,868. Local Registration of Title Office. Table 23.

Bills of Sale are registered by the Master of the Queen's Bench Division, and included in his return of business at the Plea side. They are grouped here with the business in other offices of registration. The number of bills of sale was 280, as compared with 278 in 1897, and 262 in 1896. Bills of Sale. Table 10.

The number of deeds registered in the Registry of Deeds Office in the year was 27,065, as compared with 24,817 in 1897, and 24,299 in 1896. Judgment Mortgage Affidavits are included in this number: they amounted to 744, as compared with 677 in 1897, and 580 in 1896. The searches made by the public were 6,094; those lodged for official search were 4,041, of which 1,897 were negative searches, and 2,144 common searches. The abstract book, entered up to 8th November in 1897, was, on the 31st of December, 1898, entered up to 16th December. In 1897 the Lands Index was entered to 29th of October, and in 1898 it was entered to 21st November. The Transcription of Memorials was completed to 21st September in 1897, and to 18th August in 1898. The negative searches lodged but not made were 18 in 1897, and 15 in 1898, and the common searches lodged but not made numbered 17 in the former and 15 in the latter year. Registry of Deeds. Table 22.

The negative searches made and ready for delivery but not taken out amounted to 575, and the common searches to 74.

Taxation of Costs.

The Costs taxed in the Consolidated Taxing Office, and certified, amounted to £284,820. The corresponding amount for 1897 was £276,827, which shows an increase of £8,498 for 1898, following an increase of £28,759 in 1897 as compared with 1896. Taxation of Costs. Table 24.

Administration of Property.

The number of new receivers appointed by the Land Judge (or other Judge of the High Court, but accounting to the Land Judge), was 45, as compared with 54 in 1897, 52 in 1896, 66 in 1895, 63 in 1894, 96 in 1893, 71 in 1892, 90 in 1891, 150 in 1890, 156 in 1889, 154 in 1888, 102 in 1887, and 158 in 1886. The total number under the Land Judge at the end of the year was 1,095 as compared with 1,170 at the end of 1897, and 1,211 at the end of 1896. Receivers under Land Judge. Table 26.

The year's rental under the Court of the receivers and guardians who passed accounts, which are filed in the Consolidated Record and Writ Office, is £266,831, of which £104,499 was in minor matters, and £162,332 in other actions and suits.

Central Administration of Justice.

There were 825 lettings, of which 169 were for 7 years, pending the cause, and 656 were for shorter periods. All of the lettings were by proposal without biddings.

Lunacy Department. Table 26.

The chief business in the Lunacy Department in 1898 compared with 1897 was as follows:—

Lunacy Office.	1897.	1898.	Increase, 1898.	Decrease, 1898.
Orders of the Lord Chancellor, including Fiats confirming Registrar's Reports,	610	601	–	9
Affidavits filed,*	522	531	9	–
Reports of Registrar,	106	85	–	21
Accounts, &c., passed by Registrar,	249	253	4	–
	£	£	£	£
Gross Income of Lunatics,	160,349	160,177	.	172

The number of Orders by the Lord Chancellor (601) was 9 under that for the year 1897.

The number of lunatics under the control of the Lord Chancellor at the close of 1898 was 498, being 18 over the number at the close of 1897, and an increase of 39 as compared with the number on 31st December, 1896.

QUEEN'S BENCH DIVISION—PROBATE AND MATRIMONIAL BUSINESS.

Principal Registry.

Table 27

The following is a summary of the business of the Court of Probate in Ireland and the Principal Registry:—

Court of Probate—Principal Registry.	1897.	1898.	Increase, 1898.	Decrease, 1898.
Probates and administrations with Wills annexed,	1,703	1,783	80	–
Administrations without Wills,	1,145	1,129	–	16
Total probates and administrations,	2,848	2,912	64	–
Caveats,	644	644	–	–
Causes instituted,	65	61	–	4
Trials by special jury,	5	10	5	–
Trials by common jury,	24	16	–	8
Causes heard without a jury	18	29	11	–
Court Motions,	315	415	103	–
Petitions,	74	72	–	2
	£	£	£	£
Total amount of fees received,	6,879	6,705	–	174

From the above it appears that there was an increase of 64 in probates and letters of administration in 1898 as compared with 1897, the number for which year was 93 over that for 1896.

The taxation of costs is now included in the returns of the Consolidated Taxing Office.

Comptroller of Stamps' Return as to Property under Probate, &c. Table 28.

Returns (see Table 29a and b), received from the Comptroller of Stamp Duties show the Affidavit Duty for Grants of Probate and Administration and the Estate Duty (Finance Act, 1894) received; the amount under the former heading in 1898 was £9,224, and under the latter, £500,704; the estimated capital on which Estate Duty was paid being £11,946,952.

* Not including affidavits verifying Petitions and Accounts.

From the Returns relating to matrimonial causes and matters under 33 and 34 Vic., cap. 110, and proceedings under the Legitimacy Declaration Act (Ireland), 1868, in the Queen's Bench Division (Probate and Matrimonial) of the High Court of Justice it appears that there were 33 petitions filed in matrimonial causes and matters during the year, and that these included 30 for divorce *a mensâ et thoro*, and one for Nullity of Marriage. Twenty-one citations were issued. The decrees were 9 for divorce *a mensâ et thoro*. There were 59 motions and 9 causes heard in the year. There was no petition under the Legitimacy Declaration Act. General Administration of Justice. Jurisdiction in Matrimonial causes. Table 28.

Queen's Bench Division—Admiralty.

The causes instituted in the Queen's Bench Division (Admiralty) in the year were 13, as compared with 16 in 1897, and 6 in 1896. There were 9 causes pending at end of 1897, making 22 in all to be disposed of. Admiralty. Tables 30 and 31.

The motions and summonses heard were 45, final judgments and decrees 9, and instruments, &c., prepared in the Registry 29. In the preceding year the motions and summonses heard numbered 47, the final judgments and decrees 6, and the instruments, &c., prepared in the Registry 48.

Proceedings in Bankruptcy.

In the following summary the principal proceedings in Bankruptcy in the Court of Bankruptcy, Dublin (Queen's Bench Division), and the Local Courts in Belfast and Cork constituted under the Local Bankruptcy (Ireland) Act, 1888, are compared with those of the preceding year. Bankruptcy. Tables 34 and 35.

Proceedings in Bankruptcy.	Court of Bankruptcy, Queen's Bench Division, Dublin.		Local Court, Belfast.		Local Court, Cork.		The three Courts.			
							Total.		Increase, 1898.	Decrease, 1898.
	1897.	1898.	1897.	1898.	1897.	1898.	1897.	1898.		
Petitions of Bankruptcy:										
By Creditors,	104	123	80	14	10	16	134	160	16	-
By Debtors,	16	31	18	10	1	3	35	64	-	4
Private arrangements turned into Bankruptcy,	53	40	11	13	3	1	68	53	-	13
Petitions for Arrangements,*	205	281	33	48	14	36	252	333	61	-
Sittings before the Court,†	3,011	2,801	210	680	16	11	3,237	3,025	-	212
Sittings before the Chief Registrar, and the Chief Clerk in Dublin, and those before the Registrar in Belfast and in Cork,	3 949	4,250	564	616	321	478	4,834	5,328	1,514	-

It appears that the number of petitions of Bankruptcy in 1898 was 184, or 18 over the number in 1897, which was 7 over that for 1896. The petitions for arrangement (including 53 private arrangements turned into Bankruptcy) were 333, being an increase of 61, or 32 per cent., as compared with the number for 1897, and 75 over that for 1896.

Details regarding the Bankruptcies and Insolvencies under the charge of each Official Assignee not finally wound up on the 31st December, 1898, are given in Tables 32 and 33.

* The "Private Arrangements turned into Bankruptcy" are included herein.
† In these "Sittings" Motions of Course are not included.

Finance.

Central Administration of Justice.

Accountant-General's Office. Table 37.

The Accountant-General, High Court of Justice, carried over (in cash, securities, and other effects) on 1st of October, 1898, £5,627,852:" being £192,465 under the amount carried over on the corresponding day in 1897.

Table 37 contains particulars regarding the Receipts and Payments of the Accountant-General of the Supreme Court of Judicature in Ireland, in respect of the funds of suitors in said Court, and a statement of Liabilities and Assets in respect of such funds, also particulars of securities in Court.

Law Taxes. Table 38.

A Return has been obtained from the Inland Revenue Department of the Law Taxes levied in connexion with the High Court of Justice; see Table 38.

Appellate Jurisdiction.

Her Majesty's Court of Appeal, Ireland. Table 39.

The Proceedings in the Supreme Courts of Appeal, during the year 1898, with the exception of those in the Court for Crown Cases Reserved, are shown in Tables 39–43.

During the year 45 appeals from final judgments from Divisions of the High Court of Justice were heard and judgment delivered by Her Majesty's Court of Appeal in Ireland, 25 of which appeals were from the Chancery, and 20 from the Queen's Bench Division. There were 44 appeals from interlocutory orders from Divisions of the High Court of Justice heard, and judgment delivered, including *ex parte*, viz.:—14 from the Chancery and 30 from the Queen's Bench Division. Forty appeals from other Judges or Courts were heard, one of which was from the High Court of Admiralty, 18 were Registry of Voters Appeals, and 21 were appeals from the Irish Land Commission. There were also 28 original motions heard. The Judgments delivered were 160. In 78 of these the Judgment below was affirmed; in 49 it was reversed; and in 4 varied. The Court sat on 118 days.

Privy Council, Ireland. Table 41.

There were 8 applications to the Privy Council in Ireland for confirmation of provisional Orders made in pursuance of the "Labourers (Ireland) Acts, 1883 to 1896," and there were 2 such cases remaining from 1897; in 8 cases the Orders were disallowed or varied, and 2 cases were pending at the close of the year. There were also before the Council 4 applications under the "Tramways and Light Railways (Ireland) Acts, 1860 to 1896"; and one petition under the Fisheries (Ireland) Acts.

Her Majesty in Council. Table 42.

There were no appeals from Ireland to Her Majesty in Council.

House of Lords. Table 43.

One application from Ireland was presented to the House of Lords in the year 1898: the cause was withdrawn.

Table 40.

Two cases of the nature of those reserved for the Judges of Queen's Bench Division, as to Presentments and other cases not within the 11 & 12 Vic., cap. 78, were before the Judges in 1898. (See Table 40, page 59).

II.—LOCAL ADMINISTRATION OF JUSTICE—LARGER DISTRICTS.

Local Administration of Justice—Larger Districts.

Admiralty jurisdiction :—During the year there were 4 actions or proceedings in Belfast, and one in Cork ; in the preceding year also there were 4 actions or proceedings in the former city, and one in the latter.

Local Courts of Admiralty. Table 14.

In the District Registries of the Probate and Matrimonial Branch of the Queen's Bench Division the chief (Probate) business in 1897 and 1898 was as follows :—

District Probate Registries. Table 45.

District Probate Registries.	1897.	1898.	Increase, 1898.	Decrease, 1898.
Granted in Common Form :				
Probates,	2,734	[illegible]	105	-
Letters of administration with the Will annexed,	561	600	43	-
Letters of administration—under Intestate Widows' Acts,	7	[illegible]	-	[illegible]
—others,	2,383	[illegible]	281	-
Granted under direction of Judge :				
Probates,	12	13	1	-
Letters of administration with the Will annexed,	7	10	3	-
Letters of administration,	10	10	-	-
Granted on Decrees of County Court Judges :				
Probates,	16	17	1	-
Letters of administration with Will annexed,	6	[illegible]	1	-
Letters of administration,	3	[illegible]	-	-
Total granted,	5,[illegible]	6,654	436	-
Revoked or varied :				
Probates,	6	[illegible]	-	[illegible]
Letters of administration,	[illegible]	[illegible]	[illegible]	-
	£	£	£	£
Total amount of fees received,	10,[illegible]	10,[illegible]	[illegible]	-

There was an increase of 436 in the number of wills proved and letters of administration granted in 1898, at the District Registries, of which there are eleven. This increase follows an increase of 411 in 1897, as compared with 1896. The aggregate number at both Central and District Registries (8,968) is 500 over the number in 1897, and 1,462 or 19·5 per cent., in excess of the number for 1893, since which year the number for each year has been above that for the preceding year.

Number of probates of wills and letters of administration in Ireland.

The 33rd section of "The Customs and Inland Revenue Act, 1881," affords local facilities for obtaining grants of probate or letters of administration, where the gross value of the personal estate of the deceased does not exceed £300, and by section 16 of "The Finance Act, 1894," the limit has been extended to £500. In 1898 there were in Ireland 99 towns where officers of Inland Revenue were authorized to deal with applications under the provisions referred to.

Proving of Wills where assets small, through Officers of Inland Revenue.

For Proceedings in Local Bankruptcy Courts, Belfast and Cork, see page 19.

Civil Proceedings on Circuit.

There are five circuits in Ireland, and in the year 1898 Assizes were held in thirty-three towns. The following statement contains a Summary of the Civil Proceedings on Circuit during that year.

Proceedings on Circuit.

Local Administration of Justice—Larger Districts.

Civil Proceedings on Circuit. Tables 46–50.

Civil Proceedings on Circuit, 1898.

Counties, &c., arranged in Circuits	[illegible]	[illegible]	[illegible]
Leinster Circuit:			
Carlow,	27	–	–
Kildare,	40	1	1
Kilkenny (County and City),	35	4	–
Queen's County,	34	–	–
Tipperary,	103	3	3
Waterford (County and City),	31	[illegible]	3
Wexford,	38	2	3
Wicklow,	48	3	6
Total,	343	13	15
Munster Circuit:			
Clare,	184	1	–
Cork (County and City),	380	20	25
Kerry,	208	4	14
Limerick (County and City),	136	9	1
Total,	768	34	40
North-East Circuit:			
Antrim (including Belfast and Carrickfergus),	248	56	11
Armagh,	108	1	–
Down,	118	5	22
Louth (and Drogheda),	64	3	1
Meath,	31	–	–
Monaghan,	123	–	–
Total,	683	65	34
North-West Circuit:			
Cavan,	96	1	3
Donegal,	128	4	5
Fermanagh,	93	8	1
Londonderry (County and City),	131	23	5
Longford,	47	1	6
Tyrone,	317	3	–
Westmeath,	14	–	–
Total,	882	39	16
Connaught Circuit:			
Galway (County and Town),	188	3	–
King's County,	34	1	–
Leitrim,	82	–	–
Mayo,	380	3	–
Roscommon,	80	1	–
Sligo,	61	7	–
Total,	844	14	–
Total of Ireland,	3,265	163	115

Jury Trials. Tables 46, 47, and 48.

The number of causes entered for trial on circuit in 1898 was 163, being 14 under that for the preceding year. The amount recovered, which had fallen from £6,929 in 1896 to £5,247 in the following year, further declined to £2,953 in 1898.

Appeals from County Court Judges. Table 50.

The Appeals from County Court Judges and Recorders entered numbered 3,265 in 1898, against 3,204 in 1897.

Local Administration of Justice—Larger Districts.

There were, in 1898, 4 objections to Presentments heard by Judges, and 10 special directions given.

Railway, Tramway, and other traverses on circuit. Table 48.

The number of railway traverses under the Railway Acts is 29, being 19 over the number for the preceding year. There were no tramway traverses under Tramway Acts in any of the five years, 1894–8. The traverses other than railway and tramway traverses, which had fallen from 141 in 1896 to 64 in 1897, further declined to 55 in 1898—£29,300 was claimed in the cases where verdicts were given, and £20,580 found by verdict.

Fines on Jurors on circuit. Table 48.

The memorials from persons fined for non-attendance as Jurors which had fallen from 35 in 1896 to 19 in 1897, rose to 27 in 1898. The fines appealed from in cases heard were £450 in 1896, £38 in 1897, and £106 in 1898. The fines in cases heard were reduced to £16 in 1896, to £4 in 1897, and to £20 in 1898.

County Courts.

Process served. Table 51.

Returns have been obtained from all the Process Servers (767) appointed under statute by the County Court Judges and Recorders, and whose salary is annually voted by Parliament.

The number of Civil Bill ejectments served by these officers is 13,827 as compared with 15,551 in 1897, 14,828 in 1896, 15,165 in 1895, 15,744 in 1894, 18,048 in 1893, 17,946 in 1892, 18,007 in 1891, 17,090 in 1890, 18,008 in 1889, and 25,421 in 1888. These figures show that there has been a gradual decline in the number of these ejectments in each year since 1893, and that the number for 1898 is very much below the average annual number for the ten years 1888–97. The number of replevins in 1898 was 603, as compared with 607 in 1897, 609 in 1896, 459 in 1895, 461 in 1894, 459 in 1893, 546 in 1892, 286 in 1891, 260 in 1890, 298 in 1889, and 499 in 1888, and the number of other civil bills, 184,184, as compared with 183,169 in 1897, 180,502 in 1896, 179,154 in 1895, 184,015 in 1894, 192,427 in 1893, 189,072 in 1892, 173,890 in 1891, 156,794 in 1890, 167,730 in 1889, and 199,689 in 1888.

County Court Proceedings. Table 52.

The statistics of proceedings (other than at Equity or Land Sessions, or under Local Admiralty Jurisdiction Act, or the Local Bankruptcy (Ireland) Act, 1888), in the Courts of County Court Judges and Courts of Recorders, whether ejectments, causes remitted from the Superior Courts, or other suits, have been collected into one Table.

Ejectments.

In ejectments entered there was an increase of 181 in 1898, following a decrease of 122 in the preceding year; a decrease of 101 in 1896; a decrease of 1,412 in 1895, and a decrease of 1,554 in 1894.

		Ejectments Entered.
For 1897,	. .	10,439
For 1898,	. .	10,620
Increase in 1898,	.	181

Cases Remitted.

In cases remitted from the Superior Courts which were entered below there was an increase of 21—from 853 in 1897 to 874 in 1898; the number in 1897 was 45 over that in 1896. In other suits there was an increase of 6,803—from 86,985 in 1897 to 93,788 in 1898, following an increase of 2,297 between 1896 and 1897, and an increase of 395 between 1895 and 1896. There were only 62 cases disposed of by a jury.

Ordinary Civil Bills.

The amount decreed in the County Courts in 1898 was £206,233 in ejectment cases, and £339,835 in other suits, making £546,068.* Compared with 1897, the amount decreed in ejectment cases shows an increase of £10,480, following a decrease of £18,600 in 1897, as compared with 1896, the amount for which year was £1,594 over

* Including £880 at Land Sessions, under the Landlord and Tenant (Ireland) Act, 1870, the total was £546,948.

Local Administration of Justice. — County Courts, &c.

that for 1895, and the amount decreed in other suits an increase of £39,656, following an increase of £8,791 in 1897 as compared with 1896, and an increase of £14,998 in 1896 as compared with 1895. The amount of costs adjudged to plaintiffs was £74,828, being £22,894 over the amount in 1896. Of these costs, £15,090 was in ejectment cases, and £59,738 in other suits.

Local equitable actions or proceedings. Table 52.

The Equitable Jurisdiction cases for 1898 (exclusive of Lunacy Proceedings), were 793 as compared with 772 cases for 1897.

County Court Lunacy Jurisdiction. Table 53.

In County Court Lunacy Cases, under the jurisdiction conferred by the Lunacy Act of 1880, there were 80 orders made.

Ejectments executed by Sheriffs, &c. Table 56.

A classification of the ejectments executed by Sheriffs and Special Bailiffs according as they came from the High Court of Justice or the County Court, gives the following results:—

	High Court.				County Courts.			
	1897.	1898.	Increase.	Decrease.	1897.	1898.	Increase.	Decrease.
Ejectments executed, .	386	375	–	11	1,720	2,010	290	–
Leinster, . . .	218	167	–	51	409	450	41	–
Munster, . . .	96	101	5	–	485	496	11	–
Ulster, . . .	65	91	26	–	453	549	96	–
Connaught, . . .	18	26	8	–	343	518	175	–

The ejectments executed show an increase of 279—from 2,106 in 1897 to 2,385 in 1898, following a decrease of 140 in 1897 as compared with 1896, a decrease of 85 in 1896 as compared with 1895, and a decrease of 311 in 1895 as compared with 1894.

The number of ejectments from the High Court executed was 375, being 11 under the number for the year 1897, 41 over that for 1896, 4 over that for 1895, and 97 under the number for 1894.

County Court Ejectment Suits and Executions compared.

The County Court Ejectment suits entered and lodged, which after having risen from 12,493 in 1892 to 13,628 in 1893, fell to 12,074 in 1894, to 10,662 in 1895, to 10,561 in 1896, and to 10,439 in 1897, rose to 10,620 in 1898, the last number thus being 181 over the number for 1897, and 59 over that for 1896, but 42 under that for 1895, 1,454 under the number for 1894, and 3,008 or 22·1 per cent. under that for 1893.

The executions of County Court ejectments show an increase of 290—from 1,720 to 2,010—as compared with the number in 1897, and are 96 in excess of the number for 1896, and 30 more than in the year 1895, but they are 160 less than in the year 1894, and 314 or 13·5 per cent. under the number in 1893.

Eviction Notices. Table 64.

The total number of Eviction Notices filed during the year 1898, under Section 7 of the Land Law (Ireland) Act, 1887, was 4,291, being 346 more than in the preceding year; but 682 under the number for 1895; 1,182 under the number for 1894; and 2,265, or 34·5 per cent., under that for 1893. Of the 4,291 notices in 1898, 127 were filed in the High Court of Justice, and 4,164 in County Courts.

Civil Bill Decrees executed. Table 54.

The number of Civil Bill decrees and dismisses returned as executed during the year 1898 is 26,619, of which 19,554 were executed by Sheriffs, and 7,065 by Special Bailiffs. In 1897 the number was 21,967, in 1896 it was 20,976; in 1895 it was 19,522; in 1894, 20,998; and in 1893, 24,368, so that the number for 1898 was 2,251, or 9·2 per cent. above the highest number for any of the preceding five years.

Warrants against Cottier Tenants and Weekly Tenants. Table 58.

The warrants to Special Bailiffs under Act 23 & 24 Vic., c. 154 (summary recovery of possession of tenements), were 960 in 1897 and 998 in 1898. The warrants to Special Bailiffs under 14 & 15 Vic., cap. 92, s. 15 (summary recovery of possession of tenements overheld in towns), 16,850, show an increase of 1,220 as compared with the number in 1897, which was 1,647 over that for the year 1896. *Local Administration of Justice—Larger Districts.* County Courts.

The following is a Summary of the Returns of Sheriffs as to execution of ejectments classed so as to distinguish the ejectments for non-payment of rent from other ejectments:— Ejectments executed for non-payment of rent and others in 1898 and 1897, compared. Table 53.

	Ejectments for Non-payment of Rent.				Ejectments for Other Causes.			
	1897.	1898.	Increase, 1898.	Decrease, 1898.	1897.	1898.	Increase, 1898.	Decrease, 1898.
Ireland, . .	1,421	1,438	17	–	685	947	262	–
Leinster, . .	435	423	–	12	184	185	1	–
Munster, . .	412	408	–	4	168	189	21	–
Ulster, . .	315	321	6	–	231	319	88	–
Connaught, .	257	287	30	–	101	254	160	–

From this Table it appears that there was an increase of 17 in ejectments for non-payment of rent (following a decrease of 156 in 1897, and an increase of 77 in 1896), and an increase of 262 in other ejectments.

The statistics as to the number of proceedings under the Landlord and Tenant Act of 1870, are shown in the following table:— Land Sessions. Table 54.

Cases disposed of at Land Sessions.	1897.	1898.	Increase in 1898.	Decrease in 1898.
Total number of cases, . . .	18	9	–	9
Decrees, ...	2	5	3	–
Dismisses, . . .	9	2	–	7
Otherwise disposed of, . .	4	2	–	2
Pending at end of year, . .	3	–	–	3

It appears from this table that the cases for disposal which, after having fallen from 83 in 1893 and 63 in 1894, to 16 in 1895, were, in 1896, 20, and in 1897, 18, fell to 9 in 1898.

There have been no applications for confirmation of leases since the year 1882.

The decrees in 1898 were 5, and the dismisses 2; in 1897 there were 2 decrees and 9 dismisses.

In the five land claim cases in which there were decrees in 1898, the total amount claimed was £1,755, and the total amount decreed without deducting allowances for set-off to Landlords for dilapidations, rent, &c., was £880. In 1897 the amount claimed in cases where decrees were made was £2,751, and the sum decreed was £230. Three of the cases in which decrees were obtained in the year 1898 were in the province of Leinster, one in Munster, and one in Ulster. In 1897 the decrees consisted of 2 in the province of Ulster. Decrees.

Court of the Irish Land Commission.

The Commissioners appointed under the Land Law (Ireland) Acts have many functions of a judicial character, therefore it is necessary in this Report to refer to the judicial portion of their proceedings, and it is convenient to do so here, as the questions dealt with are somewhat allied to those under the Act of 1870—dealt with above—and are mainly determined in the Courts of the Sub-Commissions which are most properly dealt with as part of the local administration of justice. *Land Commission Court.* Table 55.

It is unnecessary to give here a detailed account of the business of the Court of the Land Commission as the Reports of the Commissioners contain full information on the subject.

Law Administration of Justice—Civil—Land Commission Court.

Table 58.

The following statement shows generally the extent and nature of the proceedings under the Land Law Acts, during the year 1898:—

Nature of Proceedings.	Number of Cases.	
	First Statutory Term.	Second Statutory Term.
APPLICATIONS TO HAVE FAIR RENTS FIXED:—		
1. In Court—		
Pending at beginning of year,	11,846	18,140
Entered and lodged during 1898,	4,711	17,692
Rents fixed,	3,855	8,459
Dismissed or struck out,	1,088	2,385
Withdrawn,	231	225
Pending at end of year,	11,391	24,811
2. Out of Court—		
Agreements fixing Fair Rents,	4,244	8,634
APPEALS AS FAIR RENT, &c.:—		
Pending at beginning of year,	1,378	3,474
Number lodged during 1898,	1,636	4,187
Heard,	733	1,439
Withdrawn,	259	428
Pending at end of year,	2,022	5,804
RESULTS OF APPEALS HEARD:—*		
Decisions below reversed,	35	6
Do. do. confirmed,	169	440
Rents fixed below increased,	263	448
Do. do. reduced,	72	156
MISCELLANEOUS ORIGINATING NOTICES:—		
Pending at beginning of year,	438	
Number lodged during 1898,	143	
Disposed of,	104	
Pending at end of year,	478	

The following statements show the sums of money dealt with by the Court in fixing fair rents in the year 1898:—

(a.) *First Statutory Term Cases.*

Fair Rents Fixed.	Former Rent.	Judicial Rent.	Reduction.	
			Amount.	Rate per Cent.
	£ s. d.	£ s. d.	£ s. d.	
In Court,	74,891 1 9½	58,246 13 6½	16,344 8 3¾	22·1
Out of Court,	53,200 3 5¾	43,169 13 4	10,030 7 1¼	18·9
Total,	128,091 4 3¼	101,516 6 9½	26,574 18 5½	20·7

(b.) *Second Statutory Term Cases.*

Fair Rents Fixed.	Judicial Rent for First Statutory Term.	Judicial Rent for Second Statutory Term.	Reduction.	
			Amount.	Rate per Cent.
	£ s. d.	£ s. d.	£ s. d.	
In Court,	168,594 10 1½	127,485 2 2	41,109 7 11½	24·4
Out of Court,	121,806 1 4½	90,919 7 10¾	30,686 13 6¼	15·6
Total,	290,301 11 6	218,404 10 0¾	61,796 1 0¼	21·3

From the foregoing statements it appears that during the year 1898 "fair rents" were fixed in 8,099 first statutory term cases (3,855 in court and 4,244 out of court), and 17,093 second statutory term cases (8,459 in court and 8,634 out of court), the "former rent" of the holdings dealt with in the first statutory term cases being in round numbers £128,091, and the judicial rents registered by the Court £101,516 showing a reduction of £26,575, or 20·7 per cent. of the "former rent"; and the amount of the first statutory term judicial rents in the cases in which second term rents were fixed being £290,301, which was reduced to a judicial rent of £218,406 for the second

* The numbers here given refer to actual cases, cross appeals being counted as one.

statutory term, showing a reduction of £81,796, or 22·1 per cent. of the judicial rent for the first statutory term. Some of the "judicial rents" included in the above are liable to variation on appeal.

Land Administration of Justice—Larger Districts.

The number of cases of appeal from the Land Court to the Court of Appeal, and how these were disposed of, will be found in Table 39 of Appendix, and are referred to at page 20 under the head of Appellate Jurisdiction.

Land Commission Court.

A Return of Sales to Tenants under the Purchase of Land (Ireland) Act, 1885, in which the Loans were issued during the years ending 31st December, 1897, and 31st December, 1898, has been furnished by the Commissioners, and is given in Table 62, page 93.

Purchase of Land. Tables 62 and 63.

From this Return and those published in the Reports on Judicial Statistics for the eleven years 1887–97, we learn that the number of Tenant Purchasers in the first year (August, 1885—August, 1886), in which the Act was in operation, was 1,204, in the second 2,516, in the third 4,470, in the fourth 2,619, in the fifth 2,709, in the sixth 3,067, in the seventh 3,176, in the eighth 6,367, in the period from 22nd August, 1893, to the 31st December, 1893, 300, in the (calendar) year ended 31st December, 1894, 1,247; in the following year 202; in the year ended 31st December, 1896, 249; in the year ended 31st December, 1897, 84; and in the year 1898, 5; the total number up to the last mentioned date being 25,369, of whom 12,957, or 51·1 per cent., were in Ulster; 5,068, or 20·0 per cent., in Munster; 4,104, or 16·2 per cent., in Leinster; and 3,240, or 12·7 per cent., in Connaught. The total Purchase money for the whole period, from the 22nd August, 1885, to the 31st December, 1898, was £10,155,355, of which £842 was for Sales in the year ended 31st December, 1898, and the total amount of Loans £9,989,673, including £842 advanced during the year 1898. In the first year the average number of years' Purchase on Net Rental was 16·3, in the second 17·3, in the third 17·4, in the fourth 17·2, in the fifth 16·2, in the sixth 16·6, in the seventh 16·9, in the eighth 17·1; in the period from 22nd August, 1893, to 31st December of that year, 16·6; in the year ended 31st December, 1894, 16·9; in the year ended 31st December, 1895, 16·6; in the following year 15·7; in the year ended 31st December, 1897, 14·2; and in the year ended 31st December, 1898, 17.

Table 63, on page 93, contains a Return of Sales to Tenants under the Purchase of Land (Ireland) Act, 1891, in which Loans were issued during the years ending the 31st December, 1897, and 31st December, 1898. The Loans issued during the year 1898 amounted to £1,464,686*, the Purchase money agreed upon being £1,512,482, and the number of Tenant Purchasers 5,219. In the year 1892 (the first in which Loans were issued under the Act), the amount lent was £90,648, and the Purchase money agreed upon £95,149; in the year 1893 the Loans were £646,546, and the Purchase money £664,873; in the year 1894 the Loans were £787,597, and the Purchase money £809,150; in the year 1895 the Loans were £575,541, and the Purchase money, £593,041; in the year 1896 the Loans were £437,864, and the Purchase money £454,952, and in the year 1897 the Loans were £702,007, and the Purchase money £717,108. In the seven years combined the Purchase money amounted to £4,848,735, and the Loans to £4,724,089. The Loans for the seven years were made to 15,391 Tenant purchasers, of whom 6,314, or 41·0 per cent., were in Ulster; 3,716, or 24·1 per cent., in Munster; 2,881, or 18·7 per cent., in Leinster; and 2,480, or 16·2 per cent., in Connaught. The average number of years' Purchase on the Net Rental was 17·0 in each of the two years 1892–3; 16·9 in 1894; 17·0 in 1895; 16·5 in 1896; 17·1 in 1897; and 17·4 in 1898.

From the above summaries it will be seen that the total amount of Loans issued under both Acts (1885 and 1891), from August, 1885, to the close of the year 1898, was

* See note to Table 63, page 93.

£14,713,762, and the gross amount of Purchase money agreed upon was £15,004,110. The Loans were made to 40,760 Tenant purchasers, of whom 19,271, or 47·8 per cent., were in Ulster; 8,784, or 21·6 per cent., in Munster; 6,985, or 17·1 per cent., in Leinster; and 5,720, or 14·0 per cent., in Connaught.

Proceedings of Sheriffs.

The proceedings of Sheriffs in the year of their office 1898–99, including those having relation to Jurors summoned, and those already referred to, are set forth in detail in Tables 56 and 58.

Jurors.

The revision of the General Jurors' Lists resulted in the striking off of 51,571 out of 129,791 persons, or 40 per cent., and 22 names were struck off by Judges; there were only 75 persons added by Revision Court, including 70 in the City of Dublin.

Besides those struck off on revision there were 396 exempted by Clerks of the Peace. This gives the total number of Jurors on the corrected General Jurors' Books for 1899 (when handed to the Sheriffs) in all Ireland as 77,877 of whom 64,029 were on rated qualification, 10,597 were £10 freeholders, 2,776 were £20 leaseholders, 445 Directors or Managers of Public Companies, and 64 Harbour Commissioners.

In the case of 17,480 persons on the Special Jurors' Lists, 5,874 persons were struck off by Revision Court, and 3 by Judges, and 203 were exempted by the Clerks of the Peace: 105 were added by Revision Court, so that there was a net reduction of 5,975, or 34 per cent. When handed to the Sheriffs the books showed 11,505 Special Jurors.

The total number of jurors returned as summoned in the year is 44,102, as compared with 45,114 in 1897. Of the number for 1898, 4,781 were Grand Jurors* for Assizes, Commissions, and Superior Courts; 9,010 were Grand Jurors for Quarter Sessions; 1,010* were Special Jurors for Assizes, Commissions, and Superior Courts; 13,375 were Petit and Common Jurors for Assizes, Commissions, and Superior Courts; 14,485 were Petit Jurors for Quarter Sessions; 1,240 were Jurors in Civil Bill cases before County Court Judges or Recorders; and 201 were Jurors for other purposes.

In the following summary the statistics of all appeals at Quarter Sessions are compared with the figures for 1897:—

Appeals at Quarter Sessions.	1897.	1898.	Increase, 1898.	Decrease, 1898.
Appeals from Magistrates:—				
Affirmed,	213	236	23	–
Reversed,	156	190	34	–
Varied,	46	53	7	–
Otherwise disposed of (including cases in which there was no appearance),	106	119	13	–
Total,	521	598	77	–

The number of appeals from Magistrates heard at Quarter Sessions, as appears from the above figures, was 77 higher in 1898 than in 1897, the number for which year was 23 under that for 1896. Of the appeals heard and decided in Court during 1898, in 236 cases the previous decisions were affirmed, in 190 reversed, and in 53 varied.

Spirit Licences.

The number of licences granted at Quarter Sessions other than the annual licensing Sessions was 905, which, with the number granted or confirmed at the Annual Sessions (1,729), makes 2,634 in all, and of these 528 were on original application, compared with 445 in 1897.

* Special Jurors for Commissions and Superior Courts included with Grand Jurors, in the case of Dublin County and Dublin City.

SMALLER DISTRICT ADMINISTRATION OF JUSTICE.

Local Administration of Justice—Smaller Districts.

Local Charter Courts.

Local Charter Courts.

The following summary shows the business in 1898 in the eight Local Charter Courts, viz. :—Clonmel Court of Conscience, Drogheda Court of Conscience, Dublin Lord Mayor's Court (see note (*) page 93), Dublin Court of Conscience, Kilkenny Court of Conscience, Limerick Court of Conscience, Londonderry Court of Conscience, and Wexford Court of Conscience. There were summonses issued, 8,548, being 16 over the number for the preceding year, and 177 over that for 1896; causes heard, 2,838; decisions for plaintiff, 2,442; for defendant, 129; otherwise disposed of, 267. *Table 61.*

Petty Sessions Courts.

Petty Sessions Courts.

Table 59. Civil proceedings.

Table 59 in the Appendix shows the civil business at the Courts of Petty Sessions. The summonses issued were 113,770, being 9,966 under the number in the preceding year, and 1,495 under that for 1896, but 1,105 over the number in 1895.

Civil cases at Petty Sessions other than proceedings against cottier and weekly tenants were disposed of as follows :—

	[illegible]	[illegible]	[illegible]	[illegible]
Summonses issued,	83,754	75,904	—	8,850
Complaints heard,	46,938	41,347	—	5,591
Decrees made,	35,064	30,025	—	6,041
Warrants issued,	3,644	3,629	15	—

The table also shows the proceedings relating to cottier tenants under the Landlord and Tenant Act, 1860 (Stat. 23 & 24 Vic., c. 154), under which cottier tenements of less than half an acre, under £5 rent, and repaired by landlord, may be summarily recovered at Petty Sessions, for waste, for non-payment of rent, or for overholding. The cases for summary recovery of tenements in towns against weekly tenants, under Stat. 14 & 15 Vic., c. 92, sec. 15, are also shown.

Proceedings against Cottier and Weekly Tenants. Table 59.

The proceedings against cottier and weekly tenants and against servants, herdsmen, and caretakers in 1898, appear from the returns to have been as follows :—

Summary Statement of Proceedings.	Summonses issued.	Complaints heard.	Warrants to Special Bailiffs.	Cases in which there were stay of Execution.
Cottier Tenants. Under Stat. 23 & 24 Vic., c. 154.				
For Waste (sec. 84),	41	41	288	56
For Non-payment of Rent (sec. 85),	616	515		
Caretakers, Servants, and Cottier Tenants.				
For Overholding (sec. 86),	1,442	1,015		
Weekly Tenants. Under Stat. 14 & 15 Vic., c. 92.				
For Overholding in Towns (sec. 15),	35,708	19,203	16,950	38
Total,	37,865	20,807	17,248	94

Local Administration of Justice—Smaller Districts.

Petty Sessions Courts.

Non-attendance of Magistrates. Table 32.

The returns further indicate the number of occasions on which, in consequence of the non-attendance of Magistrates, Petty Sessions were not held. This number (234), as compared with 10,642 sittings of Petty Sessions Courts other than Dublin Police Courts, gives a proportion of 2·2 per cent.; but this proportion is differently distributed, and reaches 3·7 per cent. in the province of Connaught, as appears from the following table:—

Provinces.	Number of occasions on which, through non-attendance of Magistrates, Petty Sessions were not held.	Number of times Petty Sessions were held.	Proportion of occasions when Sessions not held to Number of Sittings of Courts.
			Per cent.
Leinster, (161* Courts),	64	3,193*	2·0
Munster, (184 ,,),	114	4,206	2·7
Ulster, (169 ,,),	23	3,320	0·7
Connaught, (114 ,,),	33	2,213	3·7
Total (610 Courts),*	234	12,842*	2·2

* Not including 728 sittings of 3 Metropolitan Police District Courts where local Magistrates cannot sit.

In Leinster the postponements rose from 60 in 1897 to 64 in 1898; in Munster the number fell from 182 to 114; in Ulster there was a decrease from 25 to 23; and in Connaught the number fell from 107 to 33. The total number for all Ireland, which had fallen gradually from 396 in 1893 to 278 in 1896, but rose to 324 in 1897, fell to 234 in 1898.

ROBERT E. MATHESON,
Registrar-General.

General Register Office,
Charlemont House,
Dublin, 26th *April*, 1900.

TABLES.

TABLE 1.—HIGH COURT OF JUSTICE.—CHANCERY DIVISION.—Return of Proceedings in the Office of the Registrars, in the Year 1896, made by the Registrars.

Nature of Proceedings.	[illegible]	[illegible]	[illegible]	[illegible]	[illegible]
1. Actions for Trial:—					
Awaiting a hearing at commencement of year	[illegible]	[illegible]	[illegible]	[illegible]	[illegible]
Set down during the year	[illegible]	[illegible]	[illegible]	[illegible]	[illegible]
Heard during the year	[illegible]	[illegible]	[illegible]	[illegible]	[illegible]
Otherwise disposed of	[illegible]	[illegible]	[illegible]	[illegible]	[illegible]
Awaiting a hearing at end of year	[illegible]	[illegible]	[illegible]	[illegible]	[illegible]
2. Motions for Judgment:—					
Awaiting a hearing at commencement of year	[illegible]	[illegible]	[illegible]	[illegible]	[illegible]
Set down during the year	[illegible]	[illegible]	[illegible]	[illegible]	[illegible]
Heard during the year	[illegible]	[illegible]	[illegible]	[illegible]	[illegible]
Otherwise disposed of	[illegible]	[illegible]	[illegible]	[illegible]	[illegible]
Awaiting a hearing at end of year	[illegible]	[illegible]	[illegible]	[illegible]	[illegible]
3. [illegible]					
Awaiting a hearing at commencement of year	[illegible]	[illegible]	[illegible]	[illegible]	[illegible]
Set down during the year	[illegible]	[illegible]	[illegible]	[illegible]	[illegible]
Heard during the year	[illegible]	[illegible]	[illegible]	[illegible]	[illegible]
Otherwise disposed of	[illegible]	[illegible]	[illegible]	[illegible]	[illegible]
Awaiting a hearing at end of year	[illegible]	[illegible]	[illegible]	[illegible]	[illegible]
4. Causes, Actions, and Matters for further Consideration:—					
Awaiting a hearing at commencement of year	[illegible]	[illegible]	[illegible]	[illegible]	[illegible]
Set down during the year	[illegible]	[illegible]	[illegible]	[illegible]	[illegible]
Heard during the year	[illegible]	[illegible]	[illegible]	[illegible]	[illegible]
Otherwise disposed of	[illegible]	[illegible]	[illegible]	[illegible]	[illegible]
Awaiting a hearing at end of year	[illegible]	[illegible]	[illegible]	[illegible]	[illegible]
5. [illegible]					
Awaiting a hearing at commencement of year	[illegible]	[illegible]	[illegible]	[illegible]	[illegible]
Set down during the year	[illegible]	[illegible]	[illegible]	[illegible]	[illegible]
Heard during the year	[illegible]	[illegible]	[illegible]	[illegible]	[illegible]
Otherwise disposed of	[illegible]	[illegible]	[illegible]	[illegible]	[illegible]
Awaiting a hearing at end of year	[illegible]	[illegible]	[illegible]	[illegible]	[illegible]
6. [illegible]	[illegible]	[illegible]	[illegible]	[illegible]	[illegible]
7. Orders made on the hearing of [illegible]	[illegible]	[illegible]	[illegible]	[illegible]	[illegible]
8. Orders made on the hearing of [illegible]	[illegible]	[illegible]	[illegible]	[illegible]	[illegible]
9. Orders made in Chambers on [illegible]	[illegible]	[illegible]	[illegible]	[illegible]	[illegible]
10. Orders made in Chambers in matters [illegible]	[illegible]	[illegible]	[illegible]	[illegible]	[illegible]

Nature of Proceedings.	[illegible]	[illegible]	[illegible]	[illegible]	[illegible]
11. (a) Orders made on [illegible]	[illegible]	[illegible]	[illegible]	[illegible]	[illegible]
(b) [illegible]	[illegible]	[illegible]	[illegible]	[illegible]	[illegible]
(c) [illegible]	[illegible]	[illegible]	[illegible]	[illegible]	[illegible]
(d) Orders made on [illegible]	[illegible]	[illegible]	[illegible]	[illegible]	[illegible]
(e) Orders made [illegible]	[illegible]	[illegible]	[illegible]	[illegible]	[illegible]
(f) Orders made [illegible]	[illegible]	[illegible]	[illegible]	[illegible]	[illegible]
(g) Orders made [illegible] County Court Appeals	[illegible]	[illegible]	[illegible]	[illegible]	[illegible]
(h) Orders made [illegible]	[illegible]	[illegible]	[illegible]	[illegible]	[illegible]
12. Number of Judgments entered	[illegible]	[illegible]	[illegible]	[illegible]	[illegible]
13. Number of [illegible] lodged	[illegible]	[illegible]	[illegible]	[illegible]	[illegible]
14. Number of (a) Petitions [illegible]:—					
(1.) Under [illegible] Acts	[illegible]	[illegible]	[illegible]	[illegible]	[illegible]
(2.) Other [illegible]	[illegible]	[illegible]	[illegible]	[illegible]	[illegible]
(b) [illegible]	[illegible]	[illegible]	[illegible]	[illegible]	[illegible]
(c) [illegible] do. do.	[illegible]	[illegible]	[illegible]	[illegible]	[illegible]
(d) [illegible] do. do.	[illegible]	[illegible]	[illegible]	[illegible]	[illegible]
(e) [illegible]	[illegible]	[illegible]	[illegible]	[illegible]	[illegible]
15. Number of (a) [illegible]	[illegible]	[illegible]	[illegible]	[illegible]	[illegible]
(b) [illegible]	[illegible]	[illegible]	[illegible]	[illegible]	[illegible]
(c) [illegible]	[illegible]	[illegible]	[illegible]	[illegible]	[illegible]
(d) [illegible]	[illegible]	[illegible]	[illegible]	[illegible]	[illegible]
(e) [illegible]	[illegible]	[illegible]	[illegible]	[illegible]	[illegible]
16. Number of [illegible]	[illegible]	[illegible]	[illegible]	[illegible]	[illegible]
17. [illegible]	[illegible]	[illegible]	[illegible]	[illegible]	[illegible]
18. [illegible]	[illegible]	[illegible]	[illegible]	[illegible]	[illegible]
19. Number of days the [illegible]	[illegible]	[illegible]	[illegible]	[illegible]	[illegible]
20. [illegible]					
(a) [illegible]	[illegible]	[illegible]	[illegible]	[illegible]	[illegible]
(b) [illegible]	[illegible]	[illegible]	[illegible]	[illegible]	[illegible]
21. Amount of [illegible]					
[illegible]	[illegible]				
[illegible]	[illegible]				
[illegible]	[illegible]				
[illegible]	[illegible]				
Total	[illegible]				

* [illegible] † [illegible] ‡ [illegible]

TABLE 2.—HIGH COURT OF JUSTICE.—CHANCERY DIVISION.—Return of Appeals from County Courts in Equity Civil Bills, and Proceedings in the Year 1897, by the proper officer under Order XVII., Rule 130, of County Courts

TABLE 2.—HIGH COURT OF JUSTICE.—CHANCERY DIVISION.—Return of Proceedings in the Chambers of the Lord Chancellor, Master of the Rolls, and Vice-Chancellor, for the Year 1886, made by the Chief Clerks to the Judges.

Nature of Proceedings.	Total.		Lord Chancellor.		Master of the Rolls.		Vice-Chancellor.	
	No.	Amount.	No.	Amount.	No.	Amount.	No.	Amount.
[illegible]		£ s. d.		£ s. d.		£ s. d.		£ s. d.
[illegible]	[illegible]	[illegible]	[illegible]	[illegible]	[illegible]	[illegible]	[illegible]	[illegible]

TABLE 4.—HIGH COURT OF JUSTICE.—CHANCERY DIVISION.—Return of Proceedings in the Office of the Clerk of Records and Writs, for the Year [illegible], made by the Clerk of Records and Writs.

NATURE OF PROCEEDINGS.	[illegible]	[illegible]	[illegible]	[illegible]	[illegible]	Total.
1. Actions and Suits instituted:—						
Actions by Writ of Summons,	[illegible]	[illegible]	.	[illegible]	[illegible]	[illegible]
Summary Petitions,	[illegible]	[illegible]	[illegible]	[illegible]	[illegible]	[illegible]
Special Cases (Act under [illegible] Vic. c. [illegible]),	.	.	.	.	.	.
Notices of Motion filed in lieu of Petition,	[illegible]	.	.	7	[illegible]	[illegible]
Originating Summonses,	[illegible]	[illegible]	.	[illegible]	[illegible]	[illegible]
Orders transferring Lunacy Matters to Chancery,	.	.	.	.	.	.
Schemes for Arrangement under Railway Act, [illegible]	.	.	.	.	.	.
Actions transferred from other Divisions, High Court of Justice,	[illegible]	.	.	.	.	[illegible]
Suits transferred from County Courts (and [illegible]),	[illegible]	.	[illegible]	.	.	[illegible]
Notices of Motion under Trustee Acts,	.	.	.	.	.	.
Total,	[illegible]	[illegible]	[illegible]	[illegible]	[illegible]	[illegible]

NATURE OF PROCEEDINGS.	Number.
2. Proceedings in Actions:—	
Conditional Writs,	[illegible]
Affidavits,	[illegible]
Searches for do.—no record kept, the number being [illegible],	.
Amendments of Writs of Summons,	[illegible]
Memoranda of Claim filed,	[illegible]
Amended do.,	[illegible]
Statements of Defence and Counter Claim,	[illegible]
Amended do. do.,	[illegible]
Replies and Answers to same filed,	[illegible]
Special Cases under Order [illegible],	.
Notices [illegible] parties under [illegible] Order, [illegible]	.
Interrogatories filed by Plaintiffs,	[illegible]
3. Proceedings in Suits by Bill, &c.:—	
Copies of Bills or Interrogatories [illegible]	.
Appearances entered [illegible]	.
4. Proceedings in Suits by Summons:—	
Copies of Summonses [illegible], about	[illegible]
Appearances entered [illegible]	.
5. Proceedings in Special Cases, [illegible] Vic., c. [illegible]:—	
Appearances entered (see preceding [illegible]),	.
6. General Proceedings:—	
Requisitions of Witnesses filed,	[illegible]
Writs of Attachment,	[illegible]
Certificates of Proceedings, &c.,	[illegible]
Attendances in Court with Records and [illegible],	.
Inspections of Exhibits, Affidavits, and Records (no Searches),	.
Memoranda entered of service of Notice of Decree,	[illegible]
Writs of [illegible] issued, [illegible]	.
Writs of Subpoena issued, and other Writs,	[illegible]

TABLE 4.—*continued.*—HIGH COURT OF JUSTICE.—CHANCERY DIVISION.—Return of Proceedings in the Office of the Clerk of Records and Writs, for the Year 18[illegible], made by the Clerk of Records and Writs.

NATURE OF PROCEEDINGS.	Number.
6. General Proceedings—*continued.*	
Oaths and Declarations administered, about	.
Exhibits marked, about	.
Affidavits filed	[illegible]
Caveats entered	.
Recognizances	[illegible]
Decrees enrolled	.
7. Documents filed:—	
Powers of Attorney lodged under Conveyancing Act	[illegible]
Certificates of Chief Clerk	[illegible]
Do. of Funds	[illegible]
Do. of Taxing Master	.
Reports of Special Referees	.
Admissions	.
Awards	[illegible]
Agreements in Compromise	.
Submissions to Arbitration	.
Statements under Law Property and Trustee Relief Amendment Act, 22 and 23 Vic., c. 35 . .	-
Schemes relating to Public Charities	7
Templates filed by Special Order of Court	.
Accounts filed	[illegible]
Recognizances filed	[illegible]
8. Orders more than 6 years old removed from Registrar's, about	[illegible]
Land Judges' Orders in Registry Cases	[illegible]
Plain and Other Copies of same issued to the Public (included in Article 9)	.

TABLE 5.—HIGH COURT OF JUSTICE.—CHANCERY DIVISION.—Return of Proceedings in the Office of the Lord Chancellor's Secretary, made by the Lord Chancellor's Secretary, and in the Office of the Secretary at the Rolls, made by the Secretary at the Rolls, in the Year [illegible].

Proceedings in the Office of the Lord Chancellor's Secretary.	Number.	Proceedings in the Office of the Secretary at the Rolls.	Number.
		Petitions set down for Hearing.	
		In Minor Matters,	.
		Under Acts relating to Public Charities,	–
Orders on Petitions as to Lunatics,	5	Under Trustee Act, 1893,	8
Orders on Petitions as to Commissioners for Administering Oaths for High Court of Justice,	8	Under Trustee Relief Act (10 Geo. III., c. 101),	.
Orders as to other Petitions referred to Lord Chancellor, including Minor Petitions,	30	Under Leases and Sales of Settled Estates Act, 1872,	.
		Under Public Works and Railway Acts,	.
		Under Renewable Leasehold Conversion Act,	1
Total Number of Orders,	43	Under Companies Acts,	8
		Under Lunatics' Settlements Acts (15 & 16 Vic., c. 48, and 19 & 20 Vic., c. 22),	.
		Under 5 & 6 Vic., c. 103, for Chancery Orders,	.
		Under Infants' Act (18 & 19 Vic., c. 43),	1
		For Receivers under Tithe-rentcharge Act (1 & 2 Vic., c. 109),	4
		For Receivers under Drainage and Public Works Act,	1
Warrants for Commissions of the Peace,	151	Under Parliamentary Deposit Act (9 & 10 Vic., c. 20),	.
Warrants as to Coroners,	–	In Infants' Matters,	1
Other Warrants to the Hamper Office,	–	In other Matters,	8
Total Number of Warrants,	151	Total Number of Petitions set down for Hearing:	
		Viz.—On the Higher Scale, 25	
		On the Lower Scale, 5	30

TABLE 6.—HIGH COURT OF JUSTICE.—CHANCERY DIVISION.—Return of Proceedings in the Crown and Hanaper Office for the Year 1898, made by the Clerk of the Crown and Hanaper.

Proceedings.	Number.	Proceedings.	Number.
Patents for appointment of Peers,	1	Writs for the Election of Representative Peers,	454
Patents for appointment of and administering Oaths to Lords Justices in absence of Lord Lieutenant,	.	Exemplifications of Orders to Lord Chancellor of England,	.
Patents connected with the appointment of the Lord Chancellor, Judges, Law Officers, &c.,	4	Elections held for the Return of Representative Peers,	2
Patents appointing Lieutenants and Deputy Lieutenants for the several Counties in Ireland,	4	Transmitting Records to Queen's Bench, &c.,	1
Patents creating Charters, Fairs and Markets, Licences for Fisheries, and other Patents not enumerated in the foregoing,	1	Number of Persons to whom Oaths were administered by the Clerk of the Crown and Hanaper, before Lord Chancellor,	40
Crown-assigned Armorial Consignments granting Charts,	18	Enrolling Deeds and Orders on Rolls of Proceedings at the Petty Bag Side of the Chancery Division,	8
Commissions of Lunacy,	1	Filing Bonds and other Documents,	1,4[illegible]
Commissions appointing Commissioners for administering Oaths,	26	Searches and Certificates,	5
Commissions connected with the appointment or removal of the Peace,	155	Proclamations,	7
Writs to supersede Justices of the Peace,	2	Recording Judgments,	
Dedimus to Swear in Justices of the Peace, &c.,	175	Commissions of Inquiry,	.
Attested Copies of all Documents registered in Office,	4	Special Commissions of Oyer and Terminer,	.
Writs of other Kinds, Mandamus, Scire facias, and other Writs,	9	Commissions appointing Notaries Public,	5
Writs for the Election of Coroners	1	Total,	2,459
Writs for the Election of Members of Parliament,	6	Amount of Fees collected by means of Stamps, £1,658 7s. 6d.	

TABLE 7.—HIGH COURT OF JUSTICE.—CHANCERY DIVISION.—LAND JUDGES.—Return of Proceedings in the Record and Affidavit Office, for the Year ended 31st October, 1898, made by the Clerk of Records and Affidavits.

Proceedings.	Number.	Proceedings.	Number.
Petitions filed:—		Appearances entered,	[illegible]
By Owners,	[illegible]	Folios copied,	[illegible]
By other Persons,	[illegible]	" [illegible]—Solicitors' Copies,	[illegible]
Final Schedule of Incumbrances,	[illegible]	Statements under Landlord and Tenant Act, [illegible] (section [illegible]),	.
Objections to ditto,	[illegible]	Schedule of Improvements under Landlord and Tenant Act, [illegible] (sect. [illegible]),	
Claims,	14	Receivers' Accounts,	[illegible]
Notices of Objections,	[illegible]		
Miscellaneous Documents,	[illegible]		
Affidavits filed,	[illegible]		

TABLE 8.—HIGH COURT OF JUSTICE.—CHANCERY DIVISION.—LAND JUDGES.—Return of Judicial Proceedings in the Year ended 1st November, 1898, by the Registrar.

Proceedings.	Number.	Proceedings.	Number.
Number of Cases pending in Chambers of Judge—		Number of Cases in which [illegible] have been had, or Declarations of Title [illegible],	[illegible]
" " at commencement of year,	[illegible]	" " Final Schedules have been settled,	[illegible]
" " at end of year,	[illegible]	" Conveyances executed,	[illegible]
" " referred to Chamber of Judge,	.	" Purchases [illegible],	[illegible]
" " for Sale of Incumbered Estates,	[illegible]	" Cases wound up,	[illegible]
" " " Unincumbered Estates,	1	Proceedings under Tenure and Improvement of Land (Ireland) Act, [illegible], viz.:—	
" " " Settled Estates,	.	Number of Statements of Landed Owners' Improvements lodged,	
" " Declarations of Title,	[illegible]	Number of Orders charging Annuities for Landed Owners' Improvements,	
" " Partitions,	[illegible]	Number of Orders made on such Petitions,	.
" " [illegible] and [illegible] of [illegible] or Exchanged Lands,		Amount of Duty paid in respect of Estates [illegible] in the Court during the year,	[illegible]
" " Apportionment of Rent,		Amount of money paid out during the year,	[illegible]
" " Specific performance of Contract of Sale,	.	Amount of Value of Estates where Title declared,	-
" " Appointments of New Trustees,	1	Net Rental or Annual Value where given, of Estates sold,	[illegible]
	[illegible]	Amount of Purchase money,	[illegible]
" Statements under Landlord and Tenant Act, [illegible], Part II.,	.		
" Building Leases sanctioned,	.		
" Proceedings to authorize Leases not within [illegible] terms of Act or Settlement,	.		
" Cases in which Titles approved of,	[illegible]		

TABLE 9.—HIGH COURT OF JUSTICE.—CHANCERY DIVISION.—LAND JUDGE. Return of Proceedings in the Deeds Office, for the Year ended 1st November, 1898, made by the Keeper of Deeds.

Proceedings.	Number.	Proceedings.	Number.
Rentals lodged,	[illegible]	Receipts for Deeds or other Documents (given up to [illegible]),	[illegible]
Deeds or other Documents lodged,	[illegible]	Orders to give out Deeds or other Documents,	[illegible]
Abstracts of Title lodged,	[illegible]		
Receipts for Deeds or other Documents (to be returned),	[illegible]		

TABLE 10.—HIGH COURT OF JUSTICE.—QUEEN'S BENCH DIVISION.—Return of the Proceedings of the Court on the Plea Side in the Year 1898, made by the Master of the Court, the Registrar, and the Clerk of Writs.

PROCEEDINGS.	Totals. No.	Totals. Number heard in Banco.	Quarter ending 31st March. No.	Quarter ending 31st March. Number heard in Banco.	Quarter ending 30th June. No.	Quarter ending 30th June. Number heard in Banco.	Quarter ending 30th September. No.	Quarter ending 30th September. Number heard in Banco.	Quarter ending 31st December. No.	Quarter ending 31st December. Number heard in Banco.
Returned by Clerk of Writs.										
Writs of Summons issued,	[illegible]		[illegible]	.	[illegible]		[illegible]	.	[illegible]	.
Writs of Revivor,	.	.			.	.	.	.		.
Writs of Registration,	.	.			.	.	.	.	.	.
Registrations, Suggestions, &c.,	[illegible]	.	[illegible]	.	[illegible]	.	[illegible]	.	[illegible]	
Examinations and Returns under Old System,	.				.	.	.	.	.	.
Returned by Master.										
Appearances entered,	[illegible]		[illegible]	.	[illegible]	.	[illegible]	.	[illegible]	.
Judgments entered:										
On Affidavit of Service (in default of Appearance),	[illegible]	.	[illegible]	.	[illegible]	.	[illegible]	.	[illegible]	.
By default (other than default of Appearance) for Plaintiff,	[illegible]	.	[illegible]	.	[illegible]	.	[illegible]	.	[illegible]	.
[illegible]	[illegible]	.	[illegible]	.	[illegible]	.	[illegible]	.	[illegible]	.
(Summary) under Order [illegible], Rule 1,	[illegible]	.	[illegible]	.	[illegible]	.	[illegible]	.	[illegible]	.
For Plaintiff on Verdict, or Writ of Inquiry,	[illegible]	.	[illegible]	.	[illegible]	.	[illegible]	.	[illegible]	.
For Defendant on Verdict or Non-suit,	[illegible]	.	[illegible]	.	[illegible]	.	[illegible]	.	[illegible]	.
On Warrants of Attorney,	[illegible]	.	[illegible]	.	[illegible]	.	[illegible]	.	[illegible]	.
On Certificates of Master,	[illegible]	.	[illegible]	.	[illegible]	.	[illegible]	.	[illegible]	.
Other Judgments entered,	[illegible]	.	[illegible]	.	[illegible]	.	[illegible]	.	[illegible]	.
Executions:										
Writs of Fieri Facias issued,	[illegible]	.	[illegible]	.	[illegible]	.	[illegible]	.	[illegible]	.
Writs of Possession,	[illegible]	.	[illegible]	.	[illegible]	.	[illegible]	.	[illegible]	.
Returned by the Registrar.										
Motions on Notice for New Trial, or to enter Judgment (Heard):										
Refused,	[illegible]	.	[illegible]	.	[illegible]	.	.	.	[illegible]	.
Granted,	[illegible]	.	[illegible]	.	[illegible]	.	.	.	[illegible]	.
Other Motions (Heard):										
Refused,	[illegible]	.	[illegible]	.	[illegible]	.	.	.	[illegible]	.
Granted,	[illegible]	.	[illegible]	.	[illegible]	.	.	.	[illegible]	.
Special Cases (Heard):										
Judgments for Plaintiff,	[illegible]	.	[illegible]	.	[illegible]	.	.	.	.	.
Judgments for Defendant,	[illegible]	.	[illegible]	.	.	.	.	.	[illegible]	.
Points of Law:										
Judgments for Plaintiff,	.	.	.	.	.	.	.	.	.	.
Judgments for Defendant,	.	.	.	.	.	.	.	.	.	.
Side Bar Rules,	[illegible]	.	[illegible]	.	[illegible]	.	[illegible]	.	[illegible]	.
Cases heard in which the Court divided,	[illegible]	.	.	.	[illegible]	.	.	.	[illegible]	.
Other Proceedings,	[illegible]	.	[illegible]	.	[illegible]	.	.	.	[illegible]	.
Returned by Master.										
Causes referred to Master under Common Law Procedure Acts, 1853 and 1856, and to other Masters,	[illegible]	.	[illegible]	.	[illegible]	.	[illegible]	.	[illegible]	.
Bills of Sale,	[illegible]	.	[illegible]	.	[illegible]	.	[illegible]	.	[illegible]	.
Affidavits filed,	[illegible]	.	[illegible]	.	[illegible]	.	[illegible]	.	[illegible]	.
Other Documents filed, viz.—										
Writs of Summons,	[illegible]	.	[illegible]	.	[illegible]	.	[illegible]	.	[illegible]	.
Statements of Claim,	[illegible]	.	[illegible]	.	[illegible]	.	[illegible]	.	[illegible]	.
Defences,	[illegible]	.	[illegible]	.	[illegible]	.	[illegible]	.	[illegible]	.
Replies,	[illegible]	.	[illegible]	.	[illegible]	.	[illegible]	.	[illegible]	.
Consents,	[illegible]	.	[illegible]	.	[illegible]	.	[illegible]	.	[illegible]	.
Discontinuances,	[illegible]	.	[illegible]	.	[illegible]	.	[illegible]	.	[illegible]	.
Judge's Certificates,	[illegible]	.	[illegible]	.	[illegible]	.	[illegible]	.	[illegible]	.
[illegible] filed,	[illegible]	.	[illegible]	.	[illegible]	.	[illegible]	.	[illegible]	.
Deeds of Arrangement,	[illegible]	.	[illegible]	.	[illegible]	.	[illegible]	.	[illegible]	.
Petitions of Arrangement,	[illegible]	.	[illegible]	.	[illegible]	.	[illegible]	.	[illegible]	.
Confirmation Orders,	[illegible]	.	[illegible]	.	[illegible]	.	[illegible]	.	[illegible]	.
[illegible],	[illegible]	.	[illegible]	.	[illegible]	.	[illegible]	.	[illegible]	.
Memorials of Assignment of Judgments,	[illegible]	.	[illegible]	.	[illegible]	.	[illegible]	.	[illegible]	.
[illegible],	[illegible]	.	[illegible]	.	[illegible]	.	[illegible]	.	[illegible]	.
Miscellaneous Documents,	[illegible]	.	[illegible]	.	[illegible]	.	[illegible]	.	[illegible]	.

TABLE 11.—QUEEN'S BENCH DIVISION.—Return of Proceedings in the Revenue, in Legacy and Succession Duty Cases, in 1896.

Proceedings.	Number.
Returned by Clerk of Writs.	
Writs issued,	[illegible]
Returned by the Registrar.	
Side Bar Rules,	1
Motions in Court,	[illegible]
Motions for attachment without Argument,	14
Cases in Information,	1

Note.—[illegible] were registered during the year.

TABLE 12.—HIGH COURT OF JUSTICE.—QUEEN'S BENCH DIVISION.—Return of Business at Chambers and before a Single Judge in Court in the Year 1896, made by the Registrar.

Proceedings.	Total in Year.	Quarters ending 31st March.	30th June.	30th Sept.	31st Dec.
At Chambers.					
Summonses,	[illegible]	[illegible]	[illegible]	[illegible]	[illegible]
Before a Single Judge in Court or in Chambers.					
Ex parte Motions (including Consent Orders) Granted,	[illegible]	[illegible]	[illegible]	[illegible]	[illegible]
Motions on Notice:					
Granted,	[illegible]	[illegible]	[illegible]	[illegible]	[illegible]
Refused, or no Rule,	[illegible]	[illegible]	1	[illegible]	[illegible]
Discharged,	[illegible]	[illegible]		-	
Referred to Master,	4	1		1	1

TABLE 13.—HIGH COURT OF JUSTICE.—QUEEN'S BENCH AND EXCHEQUER DIVISIONS.—Return of Proceedings and State of the Business as to Actions entered for Jury Trial of the Courts in the Year 1896, made by the Registrars.

Proceedings.	Totals.	Hilary Sittings, ending [illegible]	Easter Sittings, ending [illegible]	Trinity Sittings, ending [illegible]	Michaelmas Sittings, ending [illegible]
Number of New Actions entered for Trial, including [illegible] from previous sitting,	[illegible]	[illegible]	[illegible]	[illegible]	[illegible]
Number of Trials Disposed: before a Special Jury, [illegible]; before a [illegible] Jury, [illegible]; before a Judge without a Jury, [illegible]. Number of Trials Undisposed: before a Special Jury, [illegible]; before a [illegible] Jury, [illegible]; before a Judge without a Jury, [illegible].	[illegible]	[illegible]	[illegible]	[illegible]	[illegible]
[illegible]	[illegible]	[illegible]	[illegible]	[illegible]	[illegible]
Number of Actions Withdrawn,	[illegible]	[illegible]	[illegible]	[illegible]	[illegible]
Number of Actions [illegible],	[illegible]	[illegible]	[illegible]	[illegible]	[illegible]
Venue changed,	4	1	[illegible]	[illegible]	[illegible]

TABLE 14.—HIGH COURT OF JUSTICE.—QUEEN'S BENCH DIVISION.—Actions otherwise disposed of in Court in the

NATURE OF THE SUITS ENTERED FOR TRIAL AND ADJUDICATED UPON IN THIS RETURN.	Total Cases Tried.
On Promissory Notes, Bills of Exchange, &c.	[illegible]
For Goods sold and delivered, and bargained and sold,	[illegible]
For Work and Labour done,	14
For Money paid, lent, had and received,	[illegible]
For Compensation for Personal Injuries and Compensation under Lord Campbell's Act,	[illegible]
Against Carriers for Negligence,	1
Against Professional Men for Negligence,	3
For Compensation for other Injuries from Negligence,	[illegible]
Actions in pursuit of Dividends,	[illegible]
Actions in the nature of Actions of Trover or Detinue,	6
For Breach of Contract,	14
For Breach of Warranty,	3
For Recovery of Land (Ejectment),	[illegible]
Trespass to Land, Houses, &c.,	7
For Breach of Promise of Marriage,	4
Seduction,	6
Libel,	16
Slander,	4
Malicious Prosecution,	[illegible]
Assault,	7
Interpleader Issues,	7
Probate Cases,	[illegible]
Undefended Cases,	[illegible]
For Breach of Covenant,	[illegible]
For Recovery of Rent, and Use and Occupation,	[illegible]
On Life, Fire and Marine Policies,	[illegible]
Fraudulent Representation,	1
Calls on Shares,	5
Obstruction of Right,	5
Solicitors' Costs,	3
Accounts,	[illegible]
Mortgages,	[illegible]
Diverting Water,	2
[illegible],	3
Illegal Burning,	2
Tithe Rent Charge,	1
Marine Insurance,	1
Annuity,	1
Dilapidations,	[illegible]
Injury to Horses,	3
Trespass to [illegible],	3
Total,	[illegible]

TABLE 15.—DUBLIN COUNTY COURT APPEALS.—Return of Number of Appeals Recorder of the City, and County Court Judge of the County of Dublin, made by the

for Trial by Jury.—Return of the Nature and Results of the Actions Tried or Year 1896, made by a Registrar.

Class of amounts recovered by Verdict	Verdicts for Defendant	Total Amount Recovered by Verdict £ s. d.	Nature of the Suits entered for Trial and Actions tried or Settled.
[illegible]	[illegible]	[illegible]	On Promissory Notes, Bills of Exchange, &c.
[illegible]	[illegible]	[illegible]	For Goods sold and delivered, and bargained and sold.
[illegible]	[illegible]	[illegible]	For Work and Labour done.
[illegible]	[illegible]	[illegible]	For Money paid, advanced, lent, or received.
[illegible]	[illegible]	[illegible]	For Compensation for Personal Injuries and Compensation under Lord Campbell's Act.
[illegible]	[illegible]	[illegible]	Against Carriers for Negligence.
[illegible]	[illegible]	—	Against Professional Men for Negligence.
[illegible]	[illegible]	—	For Compensation for other Injuries from Negligence.
[illegible]	[illegible]	[illegible]	Actions in respect of Tenures.
[illegible]	[illegible]	[illegible]	Actions in the nature of Actions of Trover or Detinue.
[illegible]	[illegible]	[illegible]	For Breach of Contract.
[illegible]	[illegible]	—	For Breach of Warranty.
[illegible]	[illegible]	[illegible]	For Recovery of Land (Ejectment).
[illegible]	[illegible]	[illegible]	Trespass relative to Land, Houses, &c.
[illegible]	[illegible]	[illegible]	For Breach of Promise of Marriage.
[illegible]	[illegible]	[illegible]	Seduction.
[illegible]	[illegible]	[illegible]	Libel.
[illegible]	[illegible]	[illegible]	Slander.
[illegible]	[illegible]	[illegible]	Malicious Prosecution.
[illegible]	[illegible]	[illegible]	Assault.
[illegible]	[illegible]	[illegible]	Interpleader Issues.
[illegible]	[illegible]	—	Probate Cases.
[illegible]	[illegible]	—	Matrimonial Cases.
[illegible]	[illegible]	[illegible]	For Breach of Covenant.
[illegible]	[illegible]	[illegible]	For Recovery of Rent and Use and Occupation.
[illegible]	[illegible]	—	On Life, Fire, and Marine Policies.
[illegible]	[illegible]	—	Fraudulent Representations.
[illegible]	[illegible]	—	Calls on Shares.
[illegible]	[illegible]	—	Petitions of Right.
[illegible]	[illegible]	—	[illegible] Cases.
[illegible]	[illegible]	[illegible]	[illegible]
[illegible]	[illegible]	—	[illegible]
[illegible]	[illegible]	—	Diverting Water.
[illegible]	[illegible]	[illegible]	[illegible]
[illegible]	[illegible]	[illegible]	[illegible]
[illegible]	[illegible]	[illegible]	Tithe Rent Charge.
[illegible]	[illegible]	[illegible]	[illegible]
[illegible]	[illegible]	[illegible]	Attorney.
[illegible]	[illegible]	—	Dilapidations.
[illegible]	[illegible]	[illegible]	[illegible]
[illegible]	[illegible]	[illegible]	[illegible]
[illegible]	[illegible]	[illegible]	Total

* [illegible]

entered for hearing before a Single Judge of Supreme Court in the Year 1896, from the Registrars for Jury Trials (Stat. 13 Vic., c. 18, s. 30, and Stat. 13 & 14 Vic., c. 57, s. 131).

Trinity Sittings: Entered.	Affirmed.	Reversed.	Settled, Struck out, Withdrawn, &c.	Michaelmas Sittings: Entered.	Affirmed.	Reversed.	Settled, Struck out, Withdrawn, &c.	APPEALS.
								Decisions
[illegible]	[illegible]	1	[illegible]	[illegible]	[illegible]	[illegible]	[illegible]*	From Recorder, City of Dublin.
.	.	.	.	[illegible]	[illegible]	[illegible]	.	From County Court Judge, County of Dublin.
								Orders
.	.	.	.	[illegible]	[illegible]	[illegible]	[illegible]	From Recorder, City of Dublin.
.	.	.	.	[illegible]	[illegible]	.	[illegible]	From County Court Judge, County of Dublin.
								Case Stated
.	.	.	.	.	.	.	.	From Recorder, City of Dublin.
.	.	.	.	.	.	.	.	From County Court Judge, County of Dublin.
[illegible]	[illegible]	1	[illegible]	[illegible]	[illegible]	[illegible]	[illegible]	Total Number of Appeals entered.

* [illegible]

TABLE 16.—QUEEN'S BENCH DIVISION OF THE HIGH COURT OF JUSTICE.—Return of Cases of Minor Importance remitted to Civil Bill Courts, under Stat. 23 & 24 Vic., cap. 109, secs. 5 and 6, for the Year 1898, made by the Registrar.

Proceedings under Stat. 23 & 24 Vic., cap. 109	Before single Judge	Before Court in Banc	Total
Number of Applications to remit Cases of Contract to County Court (sect. 5).	[illegible]	[illegible]	[illegible]
Applications granted	14	[illegible]	[illegible]
" refused	7	[illegible]	[illegible]
Number of Applications to remit cases of Tort to County Court (sec. 6),	[illegible]	[illegible]	[illegible]
Applications refused	[illegible]	11	[illegible]
" granted	[illegible]	[illegible]	[illegible]
" giving Security for costs, and remaining in Superior Court.	Not ascertainable.		
" Failing to give Security, and so remitted, . .			

TABLE 17.—HIGH COURT OF JUSTICE, QUEEN'S BENCH DIVISION, CROWN SIDE.—(a.) Proceedings other than Causes entered for Jury Trial.—Return of Queen's Coroner, Attorney, and Master of the Crown Office, for the Year 1898.

[illegible]	Number.	[illegible]	Number.	[illegible]
Proceedings in Crown Office:		[illegible]		[illegible]
[illegible]		[illegible]	[illegible]	[illegible]
[illegible]		[illegible]	[illegible]	[illegible]
[illegible]	[illegible]	[illegible]	[illegible]	[illegible]
[illegible]				
Habeas Corpus ad [illegible]				
" ad Respondendum,	[illegible]			
" ad Subjiciendum,	[illegible]	[illegible]		
" ad Testificandum,	[illegible]	[illegible]	[illegible]	—
Informations, Criminal,		[illegible]	[illegible]	—
" [illegible]	[illegible]			
Jury Panels,	[illegible]	[illegible]		
Mandamus,	[illegible]			
[illegible]		[illegible]	[illegible]	Included in above.
[illegible]		[illegible]	[illegible]	
[illegible]	[illegible]			
[illegible]	[illegible]	[illegible]		
[illegible]	[illegible]	[illegible]		
[illegible]		[illegible]		
[illegible]				
[illegible]	[illegible]			
[illegible]				
" " by Master of the Crown Office,				
" " [illegible]	[illegible]			
[illegible]		Proceedings in Banco:		
" " [illegible]		[illegible]	[illegible]	[illegible]
" [illegible]	[illegible]	[illegible]	[illegible]	[illegible]
[illegible]	[illegible]	[illegible]	[illegible]	[illegible]
[illegible]	[illegible]	[illegible]	[illegible]	[illegible]
[illegible]	[illegible]	[illegible]	[illegible]	[illegible]
[illegible]	[illegible]	[illegible]		[illegible]
[illegible]		[illegible]		[illegible]
Writs of [illegible]	[illegible]	[illegible]		[illegible]
" [illegible]		[illegible]		[illegible]
" [illegible]		[illegible]		[illegible]
" [illegible]	[illegible]	[illegible]		[illegible]
" [illegible]		[illegible]		[illegible]
" [illegible]	[illegible]	[illegible]	[illegible]	[illegible]
" [illegible]	[illegible]	[illegible]		[illegible]
" [illegible]		[illegible]		[illegible]
" [illegible]		[illegible]	[illegible]	[illegible]
" Mandamus,	[illegible]	[illegible]	[illegible]	[illegible]
" [illegible]	[illegible]	[illegible]	[illegible]	[illegible]
" [illegible]		[illegible]	[illegible]	[illegible]

TABLE 17—*continued*—HIGH COURT OF JUSTICE, QUEEN'S BENCH DIVISION, CROWN SIDE.—(b) Nature of the Causes entered for Trial, and Results of the Causes Tried in Court, together with the Amounts Recovered by Traversers, and the Number of each Class of Amount.

NATURE OF THE CAUSES ENTERED FOR TRIAL.	Total Entered.	[illegible]	[illegible]	[illegible]	Total Amount Recovered [illegible]
Traverses in respect of Railway Compensation,	[illegible]	[illegible]	[illegible]	[illegible]	[illegible]
Other Traverses	1	1	1	1	1,[illegible]
Remaining over—Untried	-	-	-	-	-
Total	1	1	1	[illegible]	1,[illegible]

	Number.
Trials Defended,	1
Trials Undefended,	-
Remanets by Consent,	-
Remanets by Exception or Demurrer, or Points of Jurisdiction, or Points of Law,	-
Remanets for want of Time to Try,	-
Postponements to following Sittings,	-
Causes Withdrawn,	1
Causes Struck Out, &c.	-

* With [illegible] Costs [illegible]

TABLE 18.—PROCEEDINGS AS TO ELECTION PETITIONS.—Return of Petitions lodged in 1896, made by the Master of the Queen's Bench Division of the High Court of Justice.

Number of such Petitions lodged, [illegible]	COUNTY OR BOROUGH IN WHICH THE ELECTION TOOK PLACE.	Ground of Petition.	Decision of Judge: For Petitioner.	Decision of Judge: For Respondent.	Petitions withdrawn.	Petitions abated.	Costs of Petitioner.	Costs of Respondent.
							£ s. d.	£ s. d.
None.								

TABLE 19.—HIGH COURT OF JUSTICE, QUEEN'S BENCH DIVISION.—Return of Proceedings relating to the Acknowledgment of Deeds by Married Women, in the Year 1896, made by the Registrar of Certificates and Affidavits of Acknowledgments, under 4 & 5 Wm. IV., cap. 92.

PROCEEDINGS.	Number.
Acknowledgments filed, total number,*	-
Number Acknowledged before Perpetual Commissioners,	-
" " Special Commissioners,	-
" " Judges of High Court of Justice,	-
" " County Court Judges (under County Courts and Officers Act, 1877, sec. 91),	-
Perpetual Commissioners appointed,	9
Special Commissions granted,	-
[illegible] for Acknowledgments,	-

* Under the provisions of the Conveyancing Act, 1882 (45 and 46 Vic., cap. 39, sec. 7) no Certificates and Affidavits of acknowledgment are filed [illegible] to [illegible] of this Act.

TABLE 20.—HIGH COURT OF JUSTICE, QUEEN'S BENCH (late Exchequer) DIVISION.—REVENUE SIDE.—Return of Proceedings in the Year 1896, made by the Master of the Division.

PROCEEDINGS.	Number.
[illegible]	[illegible]
[illegible]	[illegible]
[illegible]	[illegible]
[illegible]	[illegible]
[illegible]	[illegible]
[illegible]	[illegible]
[illegible]	[illegible]
[illegible]	[illegible]
[illegible]	[illegible]
[illegible]	[illegible]
[illegible]	[illegible]
[illegible]	[illegible]
[illegible]	[illegible]
[illegible]	[illegible]
[illegible]	[illegible]
[illegible]	[illegible]
[illegible]	[illegible]
[illegible]	[illegible]
Warrants of Appointment by Lord Lieutenant of [illegible]	[illegible]
Writs of [illegible] under Licence and [illegible] Acts,	[illegible]

TABLE 21.—REGISTRY OF JUDGMENTS.—Return of Proceedings in the Office for the Year 1898, made by the Registrar of Judgments.

Proceedings.	Registered.	Re-registered.	Total.	Proceedings.	Registered.	Re-registered.	Total.
Judgments of Superior Courts obtained before 19th July, 1850,	.	[illegible]	[illegible]	Recognizances,	[illegible]	[illegible]	[illegible]
Judgments of Superior Courts obtained since 19th July, 1850,	[illegible]	[illegible]	[illegible]	Crown Bonds,	[illegible]	[illegible]	[illegible]
Reversals,	.	.	.	Judgments at Suit of Crown,	.	.	.
Decrees, Rules, and Orders,	.	.	.	Statutes,	.	.	.
Lis pendens,	[illegible]	[illegible]	[illegible]	Inquisitions,	.	.	.
Civil Bill Decrees for Poor Rates,	.	.	.	Acceptances of Office,	.	.	.
Judgments from Courts in England and Scotland,	[illegible]	.	[illegible]				
Total,	[illegible]	[illegible]	[illegible]	Total,	[illegible]	[illegible]	[illegible]

Satisfactions of Judgments,	[illegible]	Negative Searches on 1s. Stamps made,	[illegible]
Vacates of Recognizances,	[illegible]	Do. do. 2s. 6d. do.,	[illegible]
Cancellations of Crown Bonds,	[illegible]	Requisitions for liberty to Search made by Public,	[illegible]
Negative Searches on £1 Stamps made,	.	Duplicate Searches issued,	[illegible]

Number of Stamped Certificates issued upon which the Registrar, pursuant to 23 & 24 Vic., c. 115, received Fees, ... [illegible]

TABLE 22 (a.)—HIGH COURT OF JUSTICE.—CHANCERY DIVISION.—LAND JUDGES.—Return of Proceedings in the Local Registration of Title (Ireland) Office for the Year 1898, made by the Registrar.

Number of Applications to Register.			Number of Folios Filed.	Number of Searches Issued.	Number of Owners Registered.	Amount of Fees Collected.	
Compulsory.	Voluntary.	Total.				Insurance.	Other Fees.
						£ s. d.	£ s. d.
[illegible]	[illegible]	[illegible]	[illegible]	[illegible]	[illegible]	[illegible]	[illegible]

(b.) LOCAL REGISTRATION OF TITLE OFFICE.—Summary of Fees received in 1898, furnished by the Registrar.

County.	Insurance.	Other Fees.	County.	Insurance.	Other Fees.
	£ s. d.	£ s. d.		£ s. d.	£ s. d.
Central,	[illegible]	[illegible]	Londonderry,	[illegible]	[illegible]
Antrim,	[illegible]	[illegible]	Longford,	[illegible]	[illegible]
Armagh,	[illegible]	[illegible]	Louth,	—	[illegible]
Carlow,	[illegible]	[illegible]	Mayo,	[illegible]	[illegible]
Cavan,	[illegible]	[illegible]	Meath,	[illegible]	[illegible]
Clare,	[illegible]	[illegible]	Monaghan,	[illegible]	[illegible]
Cork,	[illegible]	[illegible]	Queen's County,	[illegible]	[illegible]
Donegal,	[illegible]	[illegible]	Roscommon,	[illegible]	[illegible]
Down,	[illegible]	[illegible]	Sligo,	[illegible]	[illegible]
Fermanagh,	[illegible]	[illegible]	Tipperary,	[illegible]	[illegible]
Galway,	[illegible]	[illegible]	Tyrone,	[illegible]	[illegible]
Kerry,	[illegible]	[illegible]	Waterford,	[illegible]	[illegible]
Kildare,	[illegible]	[illegible]	Westmeath,	[illegible]	[illegible]
Kilkenny,	[illegible]	[illegible]	Wexford,	[illegible]	[illegible]
King's County,	[illegible]	[illegible]	Wicklow,	[illegible]	[illegible]
Leitrim,	[illegible]	[illegible]			
Limerick,	[illegible]	[illegible]	Total,	[illegible]	[illegible]

TABLE 23.—REGISTRY OF DEEDS, IRELAND.—Return showing State of Business in 1896, made by the Registrar.

[illegible]	Number.	[illegible]	At Commencement of Year.	At Ending of Year.
Number of Instruments [illegible] registered in year	[illegible]		1895.	1896.
" [illegible]	[illegible]	Date up to which Abstract Book entered	[illegible]	[illegible]
" [illegible]	[illegible]	" Names Index completed	[illegible]	[illegible]
" [illegible]	[illegible]	" Lands Index (Counties)	[illegible]	[illegible]
" [illegible]	[illegible]	" (Baronies)	[illegible]	[illegible]
" [illegible]	[illegible]	" Transcription of [illegible]	[illegible]	[illegible]
" [illegible]	[illegible]	Number of Negative Searches lodged, but not made	[illegible]	[illegible]
" [illegible]	[illegible]	" Common Searches lodged, but not made	[illegible]	[illegible]
" [illegible]	[illegible]			

Number of Negative Searches made, and ready for delivery, but not taken out . . . . [illegible]
" Common Searches made, and ready for delivery, but not taken out . . . . [illegible]

TABLE 24.—HIGH COURT OF JUSTICE.—CONSOLIDATED TAXING OFFICE.—Return of Proceedings in the Office for the Year 1896, made by the Masters.

[illegible]	Number of Orders and References (Estimated).	Number of Bills Taxed and Certified.	Number of [illegible]	Amount of Fund [illegible]	Amount of Costs claimed.	Amount allowed.
				£ s. d.	£ s. d.	£ s. d.
In Master [illegible]'s Office	[illegible]	[illegible]	[illegible]	[illegible]	[illegible]	[illegible]
In Master [illegible]'s Office	[illegible]	[illegible]	[illegible]	[illegible]	[illegible]	[illegible]
In Master [illegible]'s Office	[illegible]	[illegible]	[illegible]	[illegible]	[illegible]	[illegible]
Total	[illegible]	[illegible]	[illegible]	[illegible]	[illegible]	[illegible]

TABLE 25.—HIGH COURT OF JUSTICE.—CHANCERY DIVISION.—(1.) RECEIVERS' OFFICE OF LAND JUDGE.—Return for the Year 1896, made by the Chief Receiver.

Number of Cases in which Receivers were appointed by Land Judge during 1896	[illegible]
" by other Judges of the High Court of Justice [illegible] before Land Judge	[illegible]
" [illegible] under Land Judge	[illegible]
Total number of Receiver cases under Land Judge at end of 1896	[illegible]
Number of Lettings for [illegible] years, pending the Cause	[illegible]
" for [illegible]	[illegible]
" by [illegible]	[illegible]
" by [illegible]	[illegible]
Number of Accounts [illegible]	[illegible]
" [illegible]	[illegible]
" [illegible]	[illegible]
" [illegible]	[illegible]
" Arrangements for Letting of Land	[illegible]
" [illegible] of Land Judge*	[illegible]
" [illegible] of Land Judge by Receivers [illegible]	[illegible]

* Including [illegible] under General Orders I. and VI. and [illegible] by Chief Receiver.

(2.) Receivers' and Guardians' Accounts passed, which are filed in Consolidated Record and Writ Office, by Clerk of Records and Writs.

[illegible]	Number of Accounts passed in 1896.	Rental of such Accounts.
		£
By Guardians or Receivers in [illegible]	[illegible]	[illegible]
By [illegible] in other [illegible]	[illegible]	[illegible]
Total	[illegible]	[illegible]

TABLE 26.—LUNACY DEPARTMENT, FOUR COURTS.—Return of Proceedings in the Office of the Registrar in Lunacy for the Year ended 31st December, 1896, made by the Chief Clerk.

[illegible]		[illegible]
Number of Lunacy Matters [illegible] December, [illegible]		[illegible]
[illegible]		[illegible]
[illegible]		[illegible]
[illegible]		[illegible]
[illegible]		[illegible]
[illegible]		[illegible]
[illegible]		[illegible]
[illegible]		[illegible]
[illegible]		[illegible]
[illegible]		[illegible]
[illegible]		[illegible]
[illegible]		[illegible]
[illegible]		[illegible]
[illegible]		[illegible]
[illegible]		[illegible]
[illegible]		[illegible]
[illegible]	[illegible]	
[illegible]	[illegible]	[illegible]
[illegible]	[illegible]	
[illegible]	[illegible]	
[illegible]		[illegible]
[illegible]		[illegible]
[illegible]		[illegible]
[illegible]		[illegible]
[illegible]		[illegible]
[illegible]		[illegible]
[illegible]		[illegible]
[illegible]	[illegible]	

[illegible]

TABLE 27.—IN THE HIGH COURT OF JUSTICE IN IRELAND.—QUEEN'S BENCH DIVISION (PROBATE AND MATRIMONIAL).—PROBATE BUSINESS.—Return of Proceedings of the Court and Principal Registry in the Year 1896.

Number of Probates and Administrations, [illegible]	[illegible]	Number of Probates and Administrations granted:—	
„ [illegible]	[illegible]	[illegible]	[illegible]
„ Caveats	[illegible]	[illegible] before the Judge	[illegible]
„ [illegible]	[illegible]	In the Registry without decree or order of Judge	[illegible]
„ Court Motions	[illegible]		
„ [illegible]	[illegible]	Causes in progress at the end of the year [illegible]	[illegible]
„ Causes [illegible]	[illegible]	Causes in progress at the end of the year [illegible]	[illegible]
„ Trials by Special Juries	[illegible]	Causes ready for Hearing and not [illegible]	–
„ Trials by Common Juries	[illegible]	Causes remitted to Courts of Law and County Courts	–
„ Causes heard without a Jury	[illegible]	[illegible]	[illegible]
		Causes [illegible] by County Courts	[illegible]
Other items of proceedings, viz.:—		Appeals from County Court Judges	–
Citations	[illegible]	Revocation of Probate or Administration	[illegible]
Warnings	[illegible]	All Orders in the Registry	[illegible]
Subpoenas	[illegible]		
[illegible]	[illegible]		
[illegible]	[illegible]	Total amount of Fees received	£[illegible] [illegible]s. [illegible]d.

TABLE 28.—IN THE HIGH COURT OF JUSTICE IN IRELAND—QUEEN'S BENCH DIVISION (PROBATE AND MATRIMONIAL)—MATRIMONIAL BUSINESS.—Return of Proceedings in Jurisdiction under "The Legitimacy Declaration Act (Ireland), 1868," during the Year 1896, and for Matrimonial Causes and Matters, under 33 & 34 Vic., c. 110.

[illegible]	Number.	[illegible]	Number.
[illegible]	[illegible]	[illegible]	[illegible]
[illegible]	[illegible]	[illegible]	[illegible]
[illegible]	[illegible]	[illegible]	[illegible]
[illegible]	[illegible]	[illegible]	[illegible]
[illegible]	[illegible]	[illegible]	[illegible]
[illegible]	[illegible]	[illegible]	[illegible]
[illegible]	[illegible]	[illegible]	[illegible]
[illegible]	[illegible]	[illegible]	[illegible]
[illegible]	[illegible]	[illegible]	[illegible]
[illegible]	[illegible]	[illegible]	[illegible]
[illegible]	[illegible]	[illegible]	[illegible]
[illegible]	[illegible]	[illegible]	[illegible]
[illegible]	[illegible]	[illegible]	[illegible]
[illegible]	[illegible]	[illegible]	[illegible]
[illegible]	[illegible]	[illegible]	[illegible]
[illegible]			[illegible]

TABLE 29 (a).—AFFIDAVIT DUTY FOR GRANTS OF PROBATE AND ADMINISTRATION.—Return by the Comptroller of Stamps and Taxes.

—	[illegible]	[illegible]
	£ s. d.	£ s. d.
Received in Dublin,	[illegible]	[illegible]
" the country,	[illegible]	[illegible]
Total,	[illegible]	[illegible]

TABLE 29 (b).—ESTATE DUTY (FINANCE ACT, 1894) RECEIVED AND CAPITAL ON WHICH PAID.—Return by the Comptroller of Stamps and Taxes.

Year to 31st December, [illegible]		Year to 31st December, [illegible]	
Duty.	Estimated capital on which paid.	Duty.	Estimated capital on which paid.
£ s. d.	£	£ s. d.	£
[illegible]	[illegible]	[illegible]	[illegible]

TABLE 31.—QUEEN'S BENCH DIVISION—ADMIRALTY.—2. Return of Proceedings [illegible] Year ended 31st December, [illegible]

NATURE OF PROCEEDINGS.	[illegible]	[illegible]	[illegible]	[illegible]	[illegible]	[illegible]
Instruments executed, viz.:—						
Warrants,	[illegible]	[illegible]			[illegible]	[illegible]
Writs of Summons,	7	[illegible]			[illegible]	[illegible]
Commissions for different purposes,	.		.		.	.
Attachments,	.	.	.		.	.
Subpoenas,	[illegible]	[illegible]	.		.	.
Decrees of Possession,	.	.	.		.	.
Releases,	[illegible]	.	.		[illegible]	.
Commissions of Appraisement,	.	.	.	.	.	.
" of Appraisement and Sale,	[illegible]	.	.	.	.	[illegible]
" of Delivery,	.	.	.	.	.	.
Total,	[illegible]	[illegible]	.	.	[illegible]	[illegible]
Actions [illegible] of Ships,	[illegible]	.	.	.	[illegible]	.
" of Ships and Cargoes,	[illegible]	.	.	.	.	.
" of Ships and Freights,	[illegible]	.	.	.	.	[illegible]
" of Ships, Cargoes, and Freights,	[illegible]	[illegible]	.	.	.	.
" of Cargoes and Freights,	[illegible]	.	.	.	.	.
" of Cargoes only,	[illegible]	.	.	.	.	.
" of Freights only,	[illegible]	.	.	.	.	.
" of Bottomry, &c.,	[illegible]	.	.	.	.	.
" of Proceeds in Registry,	[illegible]	.	.	.	.	.
Total,	[illegible]	[illegible]	.	.	[illegible]	[illegible]
Tenders of Bail,	[illegible]	[illegible]	.	.	.	.
Reports as to sufficiency of Bail,	[illegible]	.	.	.	.	.
Total,	[illegible]	[illegible]	.	.	.	.
	£ s. d.	£ s. d.	£ s. d.	£ s. d.	£ s. d.	£ s. d.
Amount of Bail accepted,	[illegible]	.	.	.	.	.
Amount of Proceeds paid into Registry:—						
Of Ships sold,	[illegible]	.	.	.	.	[illegible]
Of Cargoes sold,	[illegible]	.	.	.	.	.
Total,	[illegible]	.		.	.	[illegible]

*Court of Admiralty, Ireland.

in the High Court of Justice in Ireland Queen's Bench Division (Admiralty) for the 18[illegible], made by the Registrar.

Seamen's Wages.	Master's Wages and Disbursements.	Damage to Cargo.	[illegible]	* Use or Hire of Ships, Carriage, or [illegible] of Goods.	Other Causes.	NATURE OF PROCEEDINGS.
						Instruments registered, viz.:-
-	-	-	-	-	-	Warrants.
-	-	-	-	-	1	Writs of Summons.
-	-	-	-	-	-	[illegible] for different Purposes.
-	-	-	-	-	-	Affidavits.
-	-	-	-	-	4	Subpoenas.
-	-	-	-	-	-	Decrees of [illegible].
-	-	-	-	-	-	Releases.
-	-	-	-	-	-	Commissions of Appraisement.
-	-	-	-	-	-	" of Appraisement and Sale.
-	-	-	-	-	-	" of Delivery.
-	-	-	-	-	5	Total.
-	-	-	-	-	-	Appraisements of Ships.
-	-	-	-	-	-	" of Ships and Cargoes.
-	-	-	-	-	-	" of Ships and Freights.
-	-	-	-	-	-	" of Ships, Cargoes, and Freights.
-	-	-	-	-	-	" of Cargoes and Freights.
-	-	-	-	-	-	" of Cargoes only.
-	-	-	-	-	-	" of Freights only.
-	-	-	-	-	-	" of [illegible], &c.
-	-	-	-	-	-	" of Proceeds in Registry.
-	-	-	-	-	-	Total.
-	-	-	-	-	-	Notices of Bail.
-	-	-	-	-	-	Reasons as to sufficiency of Bail.
-	-	-	-	-	-	Total.
£ s. d.	£ s. d.	£ s. d.	£ s. d.	£ s. d.	£ s. d.	
-	-	-	-	-	-	Amount of Bail reported.
						Amount of Proceeds paid into Registry:-
-	-	-	-	-	-	Of Ships sold.
-	-	-	-	-	-	Of Cargoes sold.
-	-	-	-	-	-	Total

* Admiralty Act, 18[illegible].

TABLE 32.—QUEEN'S BENCH DIVISION—IN BANKRUPTCY.—Table Compiled from [illegible] of the Irish Bankruptcy and Insolvency Act, 1857, shewing the state of the [illegible] finally wound up on the 31st December, 1898.

—	[illegible]				Total.	[illegible]	[illegible]
	[illegible]						
	[illegible]	[illegible]	[illegible]	[illegible]			
[illegible] :—						£ s. d.	£ s. d.
Bankruptcies,	[illegible]	[illegible]	[illegible]	[illegible]	[illegible]	[illegible]	[illegible]
Insolvencies,	[illegible]	[illegible]	[illegible]	[illegible]	[illegible]	[illegible]	[illegible]
Total,	[illegible]	[illegible]	[illegible]	[illegible]	[illegible]	[illegible]	[illegible]
[illegible] :—							
Bankruptcies,	[illegible]	[illegible]	[illegible]	[illegible]	[illegible]	[illegible]	[illegible]
Insolvencies,	[illegible]	[illegible]	[illegible]	[illegible]	[illegible]	[illegible]	[illegible]
Total,	[illegible]	[illegible]	[illegible]	[illegible]	[illegible]	[illegible]	[illegible]
Grand Total,	[illegible]	[illegible]	[illegible]	[illegible]	[illegible]	[illegible]	[illegible]

—	[illegible]	[illegible]	Total Amount of Allowances paid to the Official Assignees.	[illegible]	[illegible]
[illegible] :—	£ s. d.	£ s. d.	£ s. d.	£ s. d.	£ s. d.
Bankruptcies,	[illegible]	[illegible]	[illegible]	[illegible]	[illegible]
Insolvencies,	[illegible]	[illegible]	[illegible]	[illegible]	[illegible]
Total,	[illegible]	[illegible]	[illegible]	[illegible]	[illegible]
[illegible] :—					
Bankruptcies,	[illegible]	[illegible]	[illegible]	[illegible]	[illegible]
Insolvencies,	[illegible]	[illegible]	[illegible]	[illegible]	[illegible]
Total,	[illegible]	[illegible]	[illegible]	[illegible]	[illegible]
Grand Total,	[illegible]	[illegible]	[illegible]	[illegible]	[illegible]

Unpublished Returns of Official Assignees to Parliament, under the 68th Section Bankruptcies and Insolvencies under the charge of each Official Assignee, not

Gross Amount of Assets in [illegible]	Gross Amount of Assets in Balance Sheets, exclusive of [illegible] on Real [illegible]	Total Amount of Assets Collected.	Amount of Assets [illegible]	Amount of Professional Fees, [illegible] Salaries, [illegible] &c.	—

TABLE 23.—LOCAL COURTS OF BANKRUPTCY IN IRELAND.—Table compiled [illegible] to Parliament, under the [illegible] Section of the Irish Bankruptcy and Insolvency [illegible] the Bankruptcies and Insolvencies under the charge of each Official Assignee,

Place where Court sits.	Number of Bankruptcies: In which Petitions were presented: [illegible]	[illegible]	[illegible]	[illegible]	Total.	[illegible]	[illegible]
						£ s. d.	£ s. d.
Belfast	1	[illegible]	[illegible]	[illegible]	[illegible]	[illegible]	[illegible]
Cork	5	1	[illegible]	[illegible]	[illegible]	[illegible]	[illegible]
Total	[illegible]	[illegible]	[illegible]	[illegible]	[illegible]	[illegible]	[illegible]

Place where Court sits.	[illegible]	[illegible]	[illegible] Official Assignee.	[illegible] Official Assignee [illegible]	[illegible]
	£ s. d.	£ s. d.	£ s. d.	£ s. d.	£ s. d.
Belfast	[illegible]	[illegible]	[illegible]	[illegible]	[illegible]
Cork	[illegible]	[illegible]	[illegible]	[illegible]	[illegible]
Total	[illegible]	[illegible]	[illegible]	[illegible]	[illegible]

TABLE 24.—HIGH COURT OF JUSTICE IN IRELAND—QUEEN'S BENCH DIVISION—IN BANKRUPTCY.—Return of Proceedings in Bankruptcy for the Year 18[illegible], made by the Chief Registrar.

PROCEEDINGS.	Number.	Amount.
Petitions of Bankruptcy:—		£ s. d.
By Creditors [illegible]		
By Debtors [illegible]	[illegible]	—
Petitions by Debtors for Private Arrangements under the control of the Court, of which [illegible]	[illegible]	—
[illegible] granted	[illegible]	—
Sittings before the Judge of the Court	[illegible]	—
Sittings before the Chief Registrar and the Chief Clerk	[illegible]	—
Number of Bills of Costs certified	[illegible]	—
Number of Folios	[illegible]	—
Amount of Costs as Furnished	-	[illegible]
Deductions on Taxation	-	[illegible]
Amount as certified	-	[illegible]
Number of [illegible] to practise in the Court	-	—
Amount of Government Stock standing to the credit of the [illegible] Dividend Account in the Bank of Ireland, with Privity of Chief Registrar, [illegible] December, 18[illegible]	Nil	Nil
Amount of Cash on this Account	-	[illegible]
Number of cases of Bankruptcy referred to Chairmen of Quarter Sessions	Nil	—
Number of Warrants issued for arrest of Absconding Debtors	[illegible]	—
Number of Orders for winding up Estates of Bankrupts by Trustees	Nil	—

from Unpublished Returns of Official Assignees of the Local Courts of Bankruptcy Act, 1857, and the Local Bankruptcy (Ireland) Act, 1888, showing the state of not finally wound up on 31st December, 18[illegible].

[illegible]	[illegible]	Total Amount of Assets Collected.	[illegible]	[illegible]	[illegible]
£ s. d.	£ s. d.	£ s. d.	£ s. d.	£ s. d.	
[illegible]	[illegible]	[illegible]	[illegible]	[illegible]	Dublin.
[illegible]	[illegible]	[illegible]	[illegible]	[illegible]	Cork.
[illegible]	[illegible]	[illegible]	[illegible]	[illegible]	Total.

Total Amount paid by Debtors.	[illegible]	[illegible]	[illegible]	[illegible]	[illegible]	[illegible]
£ s. d.	£ s. d.	£ s. d.	£ s. d.	£ s. d.	£ s. d.	
[illegible]	—	[illegible]	[illegible]	[illegible]	—	Dublin.
[illegible]	[illegible]	[illegible]	[illegible]	[illegible]	—	Cork.
[illegible]	[illegible]	[illegible]	[illegible]	—	—	Total.

TABLE 35.—The LOCAL COURTS OF BANKRUPTCY IN IRELAND.—Return of Proceedings in Bankruptcy for the Year 18[illegible], made by the Registrars.

PROCEEDINGS IN BANKRUPTCY.	Dublin. Number.	Dublin. Amount.	Cork. Number.	Cork. Amount.
		£ s. d.		£ s. d.
Petitions of Bankruptcy :—				
By Creditors,	[illegible]	—	[illegible]	—
By Debtors,	[illegible]	—	[illegible]	—
Private Arrangements turned into Bankruptcy,	[illegible]	—	[illegible]	—
*Petitions by Debtors for Private Arrangements under the control of the Court,	[illegible]	—	[illegible]	—
[illegible]	[illegible]		[illegible]	
Sittings before the Judge of the Court,	[illegible]	—	[illegible]	—
Sittings before the Registrar,	[illegible]	—	[illegible]	—
Number of Bills of Costs taxed,	[illegible]	—	[illegible]	—
Number of Items,	[illegible]	—	[illegible]	—
Amount of Costs as furnished,	—	[illegible]	—	[illegible]
Deductions on Taxation,	—	[illegible]	—	[illegible]
Amount as certified,	—	[illegible]	—	[illegible]
Number of Warrants issued for arrest of absconding Debtors,	[illegible]	—	[illegible]	—

* Including Private Arrangements turned into Bankruptcy.

TABLE 36.—HIGH COURT OF JUSTICE.—Return of Proceedings in the Office of the Accountant-General for the Year ended 1st October, 18[illegible], made by the Accountant-General.

Cash, Securities, and other Effects paid and transferred.	[illegible]	Out of Court.	Other Proceedings in the Office.	No.	Amount.
	£ s. d.	£ s. d.			£ s. d.
Cash,	[illegible]	[illegible]	Total Cheques signed,	[illegible]	
Government 3 per cent. Consols,	[illegible]	[illegible]	Amount of Cash, Securities, and other effects [illegible] Accountant-General's books, being the balance of year ended 1st October, 18[illegible],	Cash. / [illegible]	[illegible] / [illegible]
Exchequer Bills,	—	—	Foreign Currency,	[illegible]	[illegible]
Other Securities,	[illegible]	[illegible]	Powers of Attorney received, viz. :—		
Securities deposited in Foreign Company.	[illegible]	[illegible]	Registered with [illegible] [illegible] / [illegible] [illegible]	[illegible]	
			Total number of Accounts,	[illegible]	

Amount of Fees collected, . . . Nil (all fees paid in stamps).

TABLE 37.—SUPREME COURT OF JUDICATURE, IRELAND—(1.) Account of the [illegible] Judicature in Ireland, in respect of the Funds of Suitors in the said Court, [illegible] September, 1898; prepared in pursuance of Rules of Court made under the [illegible]

[illegible]	£ s. d.	Cash. £ s. d.	Securities. £ s. d.
Balances of Cash and Securities standing in the name of the Accountant-General of the Supreme Court of Judicature in Ireland, on 30th September, 189[illegible], viz.:—			
Cash (Bank of Ireland), Chancery, &c., Divisions,	[illegible]		
Cash (Bank of Ireland), Land Judges,	[illegible]	[illegible]	—
Securities, Chancery, &c., Divisions,	[illegible]		
Securities, Land Judges,	[illegible]	—	[illegible]
Receipts and Transfers into Court in the Year to 30th September, 189[illegible], viz.:—			
CHANCERY AND COMMON LAW DIVISIONS.			
Dividends on Securities in Court,	[illegible]		
Cash proceeds of sale of Securities in Court (as per contra),	[illegible]		
Other Cash brought into Court,	[illegible]	[illegible]	—
Securities purchased with money in Court,	[illegible]		
Other Securities brought into Court,	[illegible]	—	[illegible]
LAND JUDGES.			
Dividends on Securities in Court,	[illegible]		
Cash proceeds of sale of Securities in Court (as per contra),	[illegible]		
Other Cash brought into Court,	[illegible]	[illegible]	—
Securities purchased with money in Court,	[illegible]		
Securities [illegible] (Land [illegible]),	[illegible]		
Other Securities brought into Court,	[illegible]	—	[illegible]
		[illegible]	[illegible]
CHANCERY DIVISION.			
Balance of Securities in Court, amount in Foreign Currency, at 30th September, 189[illegible], viz.:—		Dollars / Rupees	[illegible] / [illegible]
Transferred into Court in the year, to 30th September, 189[illegible],		Dollars	[illegible]
		Dollars / Rupees	[illegible] / [illegible]

(2.) Statement of Liabilities and Assets in respect of the Funds of Suitors in the Supreme Court of Judicature in Ireland, including therein the Funds to the credit of Lunacy Accounts, on the 30th September, 1898.

Liabilities.	Cash. £ s. d.	Securities. £ s. d.	Assets.	Cash. £ s. d.	Securities. £ s. d.
Amounts of Cash and Securities standing to the credit of the accounts of Suitors in the books of the Accountant-General of the Supreme Court of Judicature in Ireland, viz.:—			Amount of Cash held by the Bank of Ireland, and of Government and other Securities standing in the name of the Accountant-General of the Supreme Court of Judicature in Ireland, [illegible] in the Bank of Ireland, and at [illegible], viz.:—		
Chancery and Common Law Divisions,	[illegible]	[illegible]	Chancery and Common Law Divisions,	[illegible]	[illegible]
Land Judges Accounts,	[illegible]	[illegible]	Land Judges Accounts,	[illegible]	[illegible]
			Deficiency of Cash Balance, in respect of [illegible]	[illegible]	—
			[illegible]	[illegible]	—
	[illegible]	[illegible]		[illegible]	[illegible]
Securities at credit, expressed in Foreign Currency, Chancery Division,	Dollars, Rupees,	[illegible]	Balance of the Accountant-General in Foreign Currency, Chancery Division,	Dollars, Rupees,	[illegible]

* This deficiency [illegible]

† This deficiency, [illegible]

Receipts and Payments of the Accountant-General of the Supreme Court of [illegible] including therein the Funds to the credit of Lunacy Accounts, in the Year to 30th [illegible] provisions of the Supreme Court of Judicature (Ireland) Act, 1877.

—	£ s. d.	Cash. £ s. d.	Securities. £ s. d.
Payments and transfers out of Court in the Year to 30th September, [illegible], viz.:—			
CHANCERY AND COMMON LAW DIVISIONS.			
Cash paid for Securities purchased with money in Court,	[illegible]		
Other Cash paid out of Court,	[illegible]	[illegible]	—
Securities sold,	[illegible]		
Other Securities transferred out of Court,	[illegible]	—	[illegible]
LAND JUDGES.			
Cash paid for Securities purchased (as per contra),	[illegible]		
Other Cash paid out of Court,	[illegible]	[illegible]	—
Securities sold,	[illegible]		
Securities converted (Land Stock for New Consols),	[illegible]		
Other Securities transferred out of Court,	[illegible]	—	[illegible]
Balances of Cash and Securities standing in the name of the Accountant-General of the Supreme Court of Judicature in Ireland, on 30th September, [illegible], viz.—			
Cash (Bank of Ireland). Chancery, &c. Divisions,	[illegible]		
Cash (Bank of Ireland). Land Judges,	[illegible]	[illegible]	—
Securities. Chancery, &c. Divisions,	[illegible]		
Securities. Land Judges,	[illegible]		[illegible]
		[illegible]	[illegible]
CHANCERY DIVISION.			
Securities expressed in Foreign Currency transferred out of Court in the year to 30th September, [illegible],		Dollars / Rupees	[illegible] / [illegible]
Balance on 30th September, [illegible],		Dollars	[illegible]
		Dollars / Rupees	[illegible] / [illegible]

(3.) Particulars of Securities appearing by the Books of the Accountant-General to be in Court on the 30th September, [illegible].

—	Chancery, &c., Divisions. £ s. d.	Land Judges. £ s. d.	—	Chancery, &c., Divisions. £ s. d.	Land Judges. £ s. d.
New Consols,	[illegible]	[illegible]	Bank of [illegible] Shares,	[illegible]	—
Two and a-half per cent. Annuities,	[illegible]	—	Bank of England Stock,	[illegible]	[illegible]
Guaranteed Land Stock,	[illegible]	[illegible]	Bank of Ireland Stock,	[illegible]	[illegible]
Deposit Account, Bank of Ireland,	—	[illegible]	[illegible] Co. Shares,	[illegible]	—
India 3½ per cent. Stock,	[illegible]	[illegible]	Belfast and Co. Down Railway Stock,	[illegible]	[illegible]
India 3 per cent. Stock,	[illegible]	[illegible]	Belfast and Northern Counties Railway Stock,	[illegible]	[illegible]
India [illegible] per cent. Stock,	[illegible]	—	Belfast City and District Water Commissioners' Stock,	[illegible]	
[illegible] and Dublin [illegible] Co. Shares,	[illegible]	—	Belfast Corporation Stock,	[illegible]	—
[illegible] and [illegible] Debentures,	[illegible]	—	Belfast Harbour Commissioners' Stock,	[illegible]	—
[illegible] and [illegible], &c. Railway Stock,	[illegible]	—	Belfast Street Tramways Co. Shares,	[illegible]	—
[illegible] and [illegible] Railway Stock,	[illegible]	—	Belfast [illegible] Company Shares,	[illegible]	—
[illegible] Bank Deposit Receipts,	[illegible]	—	Bombay, Baroda, and Central India Railway Stock,	[illegible]	—
[illegible] Office Debentures,	[illegible]	—	Bray Township Stock,	[illegible]	—
[illegible] and [illegible] Railway Stock,	[illegible]	—	[illegible] Company Stock,	[illegible]	—
[illegible] Railway Stock,	[illegible]	—	Caledonian Railway Stock,	[illegible]	—

(2) Particulars of Securities appearing by the Books of the Accountant-General to be in Court on the 30th September, 1896—continued.

—	Chancery, &c., Divisions.	Land Judges.
	£ s. d.	£ s. d.
Canada Bonds,	[illegible]	—
Canadian Government Stock,	[illegible]	—
Canadian Pacific Railway Bonds,	[illegible]	—
Cape of Good Hope Bonds,	[illegible]	—
Carrickmacross and Drogheda [illegible] Shares,	[illegible]	—
Cavan, Leitrim, and Roscommon Railway Company Shares,	[illegible]	—
Chilean Bonds,	[illegible]	—
City and County Conservative Club Shares,	[illegible]	—
City of Dublin Steam Packet Company Stock,	[illegible]	—
Clogher Valley Tramway Shares,	[illegible]	—
Coats, J. and P., Limited, Shares,	[illegible]	—
Commercial Buildings Company Shares,	[illegible]	—
Cork and Macroom Railway Stock,	[illegible]	—
Cork, Bandon, and South Coast Railway Stock,	[illegible]	—
Cork, Blackrock, and Passage Railway Co. Stock,	[illegible]	—
Debenture Corporation (Limited),	[illegible]	—
Dr Gilbert Company, Limited, Shares,	[illegible]	—
Drogheda Gas Company Shares,	[illegible]	—
Drogheda Steam Packet Company Stock,	[illegible]	—
Dublin and Glasgow Steam Packet Company Stock,	[illegible]	—
Dublin & Kingstown Railway Stock,	[illegible]	—
Dublin and Liverpool Steam Ship Building Company Stock,	[illegible]	—
Dublin Corporation Debenture Stock,	[illegible]	—
Dublin Corporation Waterworks Stock,	[illegible]	—
Dublin South City Market Company Shares,	[illegible]	—
Dublin United Tramway Shares,	[illegible]	—
Dublin, Wicklow, and Wexford Railway Stock,	[illegible]	[illegible]
Dundalk and Newry Steam Packet Company Shares,	[illegible]	—
Dunlop Pneumatic Tyre Co.,	[illegible]	—
Dunville and Company (Limited) Shares,	[illegible]	—
Dwyer and Co., Limited, Shares,	[illegible]	—
East Indian Railway Company Annuities,	[illegible]	—
East India Railway Stock,	[illegible]	—
Eastern and South African Telegraph Company Shares,	[illegible]	—
Eastern Extension, &c., Telegraph Shares,	[illegible]	—
Eastern Telegraph Company Shares,	[illegible]	—
Edinburgh Street Tramways Company Shares,	[illegible]	—
Edward and John Burke, Limited, Shares,	[illegible]	—
Enniskillen, Bundoran, and Sligo Railway Shares,	[illegible]	—
Furness Railway Stock,	[illegible]	—
Globe Telegraph and Trust Company Shares,	[illegible]	—
Grand Canal Shares,	[illegible]	—
Grand Trunk Railway of Canada Stock,	[illegible]	—
Great Central Railway Stock,	[illegible]	—
Great Eastern Railway Stock,	[illegible]	—
Great Indian Peninsula Railway Stock,	[illegible]	—
Great Northern Railway (England) Stock,	[illegible]	—
Great Northern Railway (Ireland) Stock,	[illegible]	—
Great North of Scotland Railway Company Stock,	[illegible]	—
Great Southern and Western Railway (Ireland) Stock,	[illegible]	—
Great Western Railway (England) Stock,	[illegible]	—
Guinness, Son and Company Stock,	[illegible]	—
Hayes, F. W., and Co., Limited, Debentures,	[illegible]	—
Henry Lyons and Co. (Limited), Shares,	[illegible]	—
Improvement Warehouse Company Shares,	[illegible]	—
Hibernian Bank Shares,	[illegible]	—
Ilen Valley Railway Co. Stock,	[illegible]	—
Irish Civil Service Permanent Building Society Shares,	[illegible]	[illegible]
[illegible] (Limited) Shares,	[illegible]	—
Junior Army and Navy Stores (Limited) Shares,	[illegible]	—
Killaloe Slate Company Shares,	[illegible]	—
Kinahan and Co., Limited, Shares,	[illegible]	—
Lancashire and Yorkshire Railway Stock,	[illegible]	—
Land Corporation of Ireland Ordinary Company Shares,	[illegible]	—
Lloyd's Bank Shares,	[illegible]	—
London and North Western Railway Stock,	[illegible]	—
London and South Western Railway Stock,	[illegible]	—
London, Brighton, and South Coast Railway Company Stock,	[illegible]	—
Madras Railway Stock,	[illegible]	—
Manchester and [illegible] Western Railway Bonds,	[illegible]	—
Martin, Mahony, and Brothers Debentures,	[illegible]	—
Martineau, J., and Sons (Limited) Shares,	[illegible]	—
Morrison [illegible] Co., Limited, Shares,	[illegible]	—
Midland Great Western Railway of Ireland Co. Stock,	[illegible]	—
Midland Railway (England) Stock,	[illegible]	—
Midland Railway of Canada Bonds,	[illegible]	—
Mine and [illegible] Railway Stock,	[illegible]	—
Mitchell and Company (Limited) Shares,	[illegible]	—
Murphy, J. O., and Co. (Limited) Shares,	[illegible]	—
Newcastle [illegible] Company Shares,	[illegible]	—
National Bank Shares,	[illegible]	—
National Provincial Bank of England Shares,	[illegible]	—
New Plymouth Harbour Bonds,	[illegible]	—
New South Wales Bonds,	[illegible]	—
New South Wales Stock,	[illegible]	—
Newry Navigation Company Shares,	[illegible]	—
North British Railway Stock,	[illegible]	—

(3.) Particulars of Securities appearing by the Books of the Accountant-General to be in Court on the 30th September, 1898—*continued.*

—	Chancery, &c. Divisions.	Land Judges.
	£ s. d.	£ s. d.
North-Eastern Railway Stock,	[illegible]	—
Northern Banking Company Shares,	[illegible]	—
Pennsylvania R. R. Company Consolidated Bonds,	[illegible]	—
Peter Walker and Son (Limited) Shares,	[illegible]	—
Pim Brothers (Limited),	[illegible]	—
Portuguese Bonds,	[illegible]	—
Promissory Notes,	[illegible]	—
Provincial Bank of Ireland Shares,	[illegible]	—
Queensland Stock,	[illegible]	—
Railway Share, Trust, and Agency Company Shares,	[illegible]	—
Rathmines & Pembroke Main Drainage Board Stock,	[illegible]	—
Royal Bank of Ireland Shares,	[illegible]	—
San Paulo (Brazil) Railway Company Shares,	[illegible]	—
Sligo Gas-light Co. Shares,	[illegible]	—
Sligo Harbour Commissioners Debentures,	[illegible]	—
[illegible] Railway and Harbour Coal Company,	[illegible]	—
Spanish Bonds,	[illegible]	—
Tedcastle, M'Cormick, and Co. (Limited) Shares,	[illegible]	
Telegraph Construction and Maintenance Company Shares,	[illegible]	
Thom, Alexander, and Co. (Limited) Shares,	[illegible]	—
[illegible] and [illegible] Railway Stock,	[illegible]	—
Ulster Bank Shares,	[illegible]	—
Victoria Bonds,	[illegible]	—
Victoria Government Inscribed Stock,	[illegible]	—
Waterford and Central Ireland Railway Stock,	[illegible]	—
Waterford and Limerick and Western Railway Stock,	[illegible]	—
Waterford Bridge Debentures,	[illegible]	—
Waterford, Dungarvan, and Lismore Railway Stock,	[illegible]	—
West India and Panama Telegraph Company Shares,	[illegible]	—
[illegible] Palace Hotel Shares,	[illegible]	—
[illegible] Building Society Shares,	[illegible]	—
	[illegible]	[illegible]
Security approved in Foreign Currency.	Dollars.	
Central New Jersey R. R. Bonds,	[illegible]	—
Central Pacific Railroad Bonds,	[illegible]	—
Illinois Central Railroad Company,	[illegible]	—
New Orleans and [illegible] R. R. Bonds,	[illegible]	—
New York, Boston, and Montreal Railway Bonds,	[illegible]	—
New York Central and Hudson R. R. Co. Bonds,	[illegible]	—
United States Bonds,	[illegible]	—
Western North Carolina Railway Bonds,	[illegible]	—
	[illegible]	—
Other Securities.		
[illegible] Title and Valuation.	—	—

TABLE 39.—HIGH COURT OF JUSTICE.—STAMPS.—(1.) A Return showing the Amount received in respect of the following denominations of Stamps for the Year ended 31st December, 1898, viz., Judicature, Judgment Registry, Registry of Deeds, Bankruptcy, and Lunacy Fee Fund, by Comptroller of Stamps and Taxes.

DENOMINATION.	Gross Amounts.	Net Amount.
	£ s. d.	£ s. d.
1. Judicature (including Probate Court),	[illegible]	[illegible]
2. Judgment Registry,	[illegible]	[illegible]
3. Registry of Deeds,	[illegible]	[illegible]
4. Bankruptcy Fund,	[illegible]	[illegible]
5. Lunacy Fee Fund,	[illegible]	[illegible]

(2.) Return by Accountant-General.

	£ s. d.
Amount of percentage on Lunatics' Estates in Year 1898:—	
Cash,	[illegible]
Government [illegible] per cent Consols,	[illegible]

TABLE 39.—SUPREME COURTS OF APPEAL.—HER MAJESTY'S COURT OF APPEAL, IRELAND.—Return of Proceedings for the Year 1898, made by the Registrars of the Court of Appeal.

I. APPEALS FROM DIVISIONS OF HIGH COURT OF JUSTICE.

NATURE OF PROCEEDINGS.	Total.	Chancery Division.	Queen's Bench Division.
1. *Appeals from Final Judgments:*			
Awaiting Judgment,	[illegible]	[illegible]	.
Awaiting a hearing at commencement of year,	[illegible]	[illegible]	[illegible]
Set down during the year,	[illegible]	[illegible]	[illegible]
Heard and Judgment delivered, during the year,	[illegible]	[illegible]	[illegible]
Otherwise disposed of, including cases awaiting Judgment at commencement of year,	[illegible]	[illegible]	[illegible]
Awaiting a hearing at end of year,	[illegible]	[illegible]	[illegible]
Awaiting Judgment,	[illegible]	[illegible]	1
2. *Appeals from Interlocutory Orders:*			
Awaiting a hearing at commencement of year,	[illegible]	[illegible]	[illegible]
Set down during the year, including ex parte,	[illegible]	[illegible]	[illegible]
Heard and Judgment delivered during the year, including ex parte,	[illegible]	11	[illegible]
Otherwise disposed of,	[illegible]	[illegible]	[illegible]
Awaiting a hearing at end of year,	[illegible]	.	[illegible]
Awaiting Judgment at end of year,	1	1	.
Ex parte, already included under set down and heard,	[illegible]	.	[illegible]
3. *Original Motions:*			
Awaiting a hearing at commencement of year,	[illegible]	[illegible]	.
Heard during the year,	[illegible]	[illegible]	[illegible]
Otherwise disposed of,	.	.	.
Awaiting a hearing at end of year,	.	.	.

II. APPEALS FROM OTHER COURTS.

NATURE OF PROCEEDINGS.	Total.	High Court of Admiralty.	Registry of Tenant Appeals.	Local Bankruptcy Courts.	Irish Land Commission.
4. *Appeals:*					
Awaiting Judgment at commencement of year,	.		.	.	.
Awaiting a hearing at commencement of year,	[illegible]	[illegible]	.	.	[illegible]
Set down during the year,	[illegible]	.	[illegible]	[illegible]	[illegible]
Heard during the year,	[illegible]	[illegible]	[illegible]	.	[illegible]
Otherwise disposed of,	[illegible]	.	[illegible]	[illegible]	[illegible]
Awaiting a hearing at end of year,	[illegible]		.	.	[illegible]
Awaiting Judgment at end of year,	.			.	.
5. *Original Motions:*					
Awaiting a hearing at commencement of year,	.	.	.	.	.
Heard during the year,	[illegible]	.	.	[illegible]	[illegible]
Otherwise disposed of,	.	.	.	.	.
Awaiting a hearing at end of year,	.	.	.	.	.

III. RESULTS OF APPEALS.

DIVISION OR COURT FROM WHICH APPEAL BROUGHT.	Judgments Delivered during year.	Judgment below Affirmed.	Judgment below Varied.	Judgment below Reversed.	Cases Remanded for further Inquiry.	Judgment below Reversed, with Declaration, Direction, or Finding.
6. Chancery Division,	[illegible]	[illegible]	[illegible]	11	.	-
Queen's Bench Division,	[illegible]	[illegible]		[illegible]	.	-
High Court of Admiralty,	[illegible]	-	.	[illegible]	.	-
Registry of Tenant Appeals,	[illegible]	[illegible]	.	[illegible]	.	-
Land Cases reserved,	-	-	.	.	.	-
Irish Land Commission,	[illegible]	[illegible]	.	[illegible]	.	.
Local Bankruptcy Courts,	-	.	.	.	.	.
Total delivered,	[illegible]	[illegible]	[illegible]	[illegible]	.	.

7. Number of Days on which Court of Appeal sat, ... [illegible]

TABLE 40.—SUPREME COURTS OF APPEAL.—Cases Reserved for the Judges of Queen's Bench Division, as to Presentment and other Cases not within the 11 & 12 Vic., c. 78, in the Year 1898. By the Master of the Crown Office, Queen's Bench Division.

No.	Name of Case.	Question [illegible].	[illegible]
1	Tipperary Presentment—[illegible] Spring Assizes, 1898.	Sub-Sheriff's Expenses under [illegible] (Ireland) Act, [illegible], [illegible] Vic., ch. [illegible].	Presentment affirmed—The Judges being of opinion "[illegible]"
6	[illegible] Presentment—[illegible] Assizes, 1898. The Ballinamore and Ballyconnell Navigation Trustees.	The Acts [illegible] Vic., ch. [illegible], s. [illegible]; [illegible] Vic., ch. [illegible].	Application to be [illegible]. The Judges being of opinion the Presentments are [illegible]
2			

TABLE 41.—SUPREME COURTS OF APPEAL.—PRIVY COUNCIL IN IRELAND.—Return of Judicial Proceedings of the Privy Council in the Year 1898.

Nature of Proceedings.	No.	Remaining from 1897.	Result.—Applications or Appeals.—Granted.	Refused.	Withdrawn.	By Law, Order, etc., Confirmed.	By-Law, Order, etc., Disallowed or Varied.	Pending at close of Year.
Applications under the Tramways and Light Railways (Ireland) Acts, [illegible] to [illegible]	3	1	1	.	.	.	.	1
Applications to confirm Provisional Orders made in pursuance of the Labourers (Ireland) Acts, [illegible] to [illegible]	8	1					1	1
Petitions under the Fisheries (Ireland) Acts	.	1						

TABLE 42.—SUPREME COURT OF APPEAL.—APPEALS BEFORE HER MAJESTY IN COUNCIL.—Return of the Proceedings of the Judicial Committee of Privy Council in the Year 1898.

Cause.	Petition Lodged.	Referred to.	Cases Appealed from.	How disposed of.
Nil.	Nil.	Nil.	Nil.	Nil.

TABLE 43.—SUPREME COURT OF APPEAL.—HOUSE OF LORDS.—Return of Appeals from Ireland for the year 1898. Made by the Clerk of the Parliaments.

[illegible]	Total
Number of Applications presented in matters of:—	
Real Property,	—
Personal Property,	1
Miscellaneous,	
Total,	1
Causes withdrawn,	1
Do. dismissed for want of prosecution,	—
Judgments Delivered in 1898:—	
Causes affirmed,	
Do. reversed,	—
Total,	—
Total number of effective causes remaining for hearing,	—
Fees,	[illegible] 1 5

TABLE 44.—LOCAL COURTS OF ADMIRALTY.—Proceedings in the Year 1898. Return made by the Registrar.

Place where Court held.	Total Number of Admiralty Actions or Proceedings.	[illegible] of Vessels.	Final [illegible].	Amount of Claims.	Amount of [illegible] Costs allowed.	Seamen's Wages: Paid under Order of Court.	Seamen's Wages: [illegible] at end of year.	[illegible]	[illegible] of Sale.
				£ s. d.	£ s. d.	£ s. d.	£ s. d.		
1. Dublin,	[illegible]	[illegible]	[illegible]	[illegible]		[illegible]	[illegible]	[illegible]	
2. [illegible]	[illegible]	[illegible]	[illegible]	[illegible]	Nil	[illegible]	[illegible]	[illegible]	

TABLE 45.—HIGH COURT OF JUSTICE.—QUEEN'S BENCH DIVISION (PROBATE AND MATRIMONIAL).—LOCAL PROBATE BUSINESS.—Table of Proceedings before the District Registrars in the Year 1898, and of the Amount of Probate Duty received, from Returns made by the District Registrars.

District Registries.	Total Number of Grants issued in Year.	Granted in Common Form: Probates.	Letters of Administration with the Will annexed.	Letters of Administration: [illegible]	Letters of Administration: Other.	Granted under [illegible]: Probates.	Letters of Administration with the Will annexed.	Letters of Administration.	Refused under direction of [illegible]: Probates.	Letters of Administration.
Armagh,	[illegible]	[illegible]	[illegible]	1	[illegible]	[illegible]	[illegible]	[illegible]	.	.
Ballina,	[illegible]	[illegible]	[illegible]	.	[illegible]	[illegible]	[illegible]	[illegible]	.	.
Belfast,	[illegible]	[illegible]	[illegible]	.	[illegible]	[illegible]	.	.	.	.
Cavan,	[illegible]	[illegible]	[illegible]	.	[illegible]	[illegible]	[illegible]	.	.	.
Cork,	[illegible]	[illegible]	[illegible]	.	[illegible]	.	.	.	.	.
Kilkenny,	[illegible]	[illegible]	[illegible]	.	[illegible]	.	.	.	.	.
Limerick,	[illegible]	[illegible]	[illegible]	.	[illegible]	[illegible]	.	.	.	.
Londonderry,	[illegible]	[illegible]	[illegible]	.	[illegible]	[illegible]	[illegible]	[illegible]	.	.
Mullingar,	[illegible]	[illegible]	[illegible]	.	[illegible]	.	.	.	.	.
Tuam,	[illegible]	[illegible]	[illegible]	.	[illegible]	[illegible]	.	[illegible]	.	[illegible]
Waterford,	[illegible]	[illegible]	[illegible]	[illegible]	[illegible]	.	[illegible]	[illegible]	.	.
Total,	[illegible]	[illegible]	[illegible]	[illegible]	[illegible]	[illegible]	[illegible]	[illegible]	.	[illegible]

District Registries.	Granted on Decree of Court [illegible]: Probates.	Letters of Administration with the Will annexed.	Letters of Administration.	[illegible]: [illegible]	[illegible]	[illegible]	[illegible]	[illegible]	[illegible]	Amount of Probate Duty [illegible]
							£ s. d.	£ s. d.	£ s. d.	£ s. d.
Armagh,	[illegible]	[illegible]	[illegible]	[illegible]	.	[illegible]	[illegible]	[illegible]	[illegible]	[illegible]
Ballina,	.	[illegible]	.	.	[illegible]	[illegible]	[illegible]	[illegible]	[illegible]	[illegible]
Belfast,	.	[illegible]	.	.	[illegible]	[illegible]	[illegible]	[illegible]	[illegible]	[illegible]
Cavan,	[illegible]	[illegible]	.	.	.	[illegible]	[illegible]	[illegible]	[illegible]	[illegible]
Cork,	[illegible]	[illegible]	.	[illegible]	[illegible]	[illegible]	[illegible]	[illegible]	[illegible]	[illegible]
Kilkenny,	[illegible]	[illegible]	.	.	.	[illegible]	[illegible]	[illegible]	[illegible]	[illegible]
Limerick,	[illegible]	.	.	.	[illegible]	[illegible]	[illegible]	[illegible]	[illegible]	[illegible]
Londonderry,	[illegible]	[illegible]	[illegible]	.	.	[illegible]	[illegible]	[illegible]	[illegible]	[illegible]
Mullingar,	[illegible]	.	.	.	.	[illegible]	[illegible]	[illegible]	[illegible]	[illegible]
Tuam,	[illegible]	[illegible]	.	.	[illegible]	[illegible]	[illegible]	[illegible]	[illegible]	[illegible]
Waterford,	.	.	.	.	.	[illegible]	[illegible]	[illegible]	[illegible]	[illegible]
Total,	[illegible]	[illegible]	[illegible]	[illegible]	[illegible]	[illegible]	[illegible]	[illegible]	[illegible]	[illegible]

TABLE 46.—HIGH COURT OF JUSTICE.—PROCEEDINGS ON CIRCUIT.—Proceedings in Causes entered for Trial in the Chancery and Queen's Bench Divisions, on Circuit, in the Year [illegible], from Returns made by Judges' Registrars.

Counties and Counties of Cities and of Towns arranged in Circuits.	Total Causes Entered for Trial.	Causes [illegible] and Tried.		[illegible]				
		[illegible]		[illegible]				
		[illegible]	Undefended.	[illegible] by [illegible]	[illegible] by [illegible]	[illegible] by want of [illegible]	[illegible]	[illegible]
Leinster Circuit:								
Carlow,	.	.	.	.	.	.		.
Kildare,	1	1	.	.	.	.		.
Kilkenny,	[illegible]	[illegible]	.	.	.	.		.
Kilkenny City,	[illegible]	[illegible]	.	.	.	.		.
Queen's County,	.	.	.	.	.	.		.
Tipperary, N.R.,								
Tipperary, S.R.,	[illegible]	3	.	.	.	.		.
Waterford,	.	.	.	.	.	.		.
Waterford City,	1	1	.	.	.	.		.
Wexford,	3	3	.	.	.	.	.	.
Wicklow,	4	3	.	.	.	.	1	.
Total,	[illegible]	[illegible]	.	.	.	.	1	.
Munster Circuit:								
Clare,	1	1	.	.	.	.	.	.
Cork,	[illegible]	[illegible]	.	.	.	.	.	.
Cork City,	[illegible]	[illegible]	.	.	.	.	[illegible]	.
Kerry,	[illegible]	1	.	.	[illegible]	1	.	.
Limerick,	7	[illegible]	.	.	.	1	.	.
Limerick City,	[illegible]	2	.	.	.	.	.	.
Total,	[illegible]	[illegible]	.	.	1	[illegible]	[illegible]	.
North-East Circuit:								
Antrim,	[illegible]	[illegible]	[illegible]	.	.	.	[illegible]	1
Armagh,	1	1	.	.	.	.	.	.
Carrickfergus Town,	.	.	.	.	.	.	.	.
Down,	[illegible]	[illegible]	.	.	.	.	.	.
Louth,	[illegible]	[illegible]	.	.	.	.	[illegible]	.
Drogheda Town,	.	.	.	.	.	.	.	.
Meath,	.	.	.	.	.	.	.	.
Monaghan,	.	.	.	.	.	.	.	.
Total,	[illegible]	[illegible]	[illegible]	.	.	.	[illegible]	[illegible]
North-West Circuit:								
Cavan,	[illegible]	[illegible]	.	.	.	.		.
Donegal,	[illegible]	[illegible]	[illegible]	.	.	.		1
Fermanagh,	[illegible]	[illegible]	.	.	.	.		.
Londonderry, County and City,	[illegible]	[illegible]	[illegible]	.	.	.	1	.
Longford,	1	1	.	.	.	.	.	.
Tyrone,	[illegible]	[illegible]	.	.	.	.	.	.
Westmeath,	.	.	.	.	.	.	.	.
Total,	[illegible]	[illegible]	[illegible]	.	.	.	1	1
Connaught Circuit:								
Galway,	2	1	.	.	.	.	1	
Galway Town,	.	.	.	.	.	.	.	
King's County,	1	1	.	.	.	.	.	
Leitrim,	.	.	.	.	.	.	.	.
Mayo,	[illegible]	[illegible]	.	.	.	.	.	.
Roscommon,	1	1	.	.	.	.	.	.
Sligo,	[illegible]	[illegible]	.	.	.	.	.	.
Total,	[illegible]	[illegible]	.	.	.	.	1	.
TOTAL OF IRELAND,	[illegible]	[illegible]	[illegible]	.	1	[illegible]	[illegible]	[illegible]

Note.—The above Table does not include Appeals from County Court Judges, Traverses under the Railways (Ireland) Acts and Grand Jury Acts, nor objections to Grand Jury Presentments, which will be found in Tables 49 and 50 of this Report.

TABLE 47.—HIGH COURT OF JUSTICE—PROCEEDINGS ON CIRCUIT.—Nature

from Returns made

Nature of the Actions entered for Trial and accounted for in this Return	[illegible]	[illegible]			[illegible]	
		[illegible]	[illegible]	[illegible]	[illegible]	[illegible]
On Promissory Notes, Bills of Exchange, &c.	[illegible]		[illegible]		[illegible]	[illegible]
On Bonds,	[illegible]		[illegible]		[illegible]	[illegible]
For Goods sold and delivered,	[illegible]		[illegible]		[illegible]	[illegible]
For Work and Labour done,	[illegible]		[illegible]		[illegible]	[illegible]
For Money paid, advanced, or lent,	[illegible]		[illegible]		[illegible]	[illegible]
For Money received,	[illegible]		[illegible]		[illegible]	[illegible]
For Compensation for Personal Injuries and Compensation under Lord Campbell's Act,	[illegible]		[illegible]		[illegible]	[illegible]
Against Carriers for Negligence,	[illegible]		[illegible]			.
Against Professional Men for Negligence,	[illegible]		[illegible]		[illegible]	.
For Compensation for other Injuries from Negligence,	[illegible]	.	[illegible]		[illegible]	[illegible]
Actions in the nature of Actions of Trover or Detinue,	[illegible]	.	[illegible]		[illegible]	[illegible]
For Breach of Contract,	[illegible]	.	[illegible]		[illegible]	[illegible]
For Breach of Warranty,	[illegible]	.	[illegible]	.	[illegible]	[illegible]
For Recovery of Land (Ejectment),	[illegible]	.	[illegible]	.	[illegible]	[illegible]
Trespass relative to Land, Houses, &c.	[illegible]	.	[illegible]	.	[illegible]	[illegible]
For Breach of Promise of Marriage,	[illegible]	.	[illegible]	.	[illegible]	[illegible]
Seduction,	[illegible]	.	[illegible]	.	[illegible]	[illegible]
Libel,	[illegible]	.	[illegible]	.	[illegible]	[illegible]
Slander,	[illegible]	.	[illegible]	.	[illegible]	[illegible]
Malicious Prosecution,	[illegible]	.	[illegible]	.	[illegible]	[illegible]
Assault,	[illegible]	.	[illegible]	.	[illegible]	[illegible]
Interpleader Issues,	[illegible]	.	[illegible]	.	[illegible]	.
Issues from Courts of Equity,	[illegible]	.	[illegible]	.	[illegible]	.
For Breach of Covenant,	[illegible]	.	[illegible]	.	[illegible]	[illegible]
For Recovery of Rent,	[illegible]	.	[illegible]	.	[illegible]	.
Right of Way,	[illegible]	.	[illegible]	.	[illegible]	.
Probate of Will,	[illegible]	.	.	[illegible]	[illegible]	[illegible]
Divorce,	[illegible]	.	.	[illegible]	[illegible]	[illegible]
Wrongful Dismissal,	[illegible]		[illegible]	.	[illegible]	[illegible]
[illegible]	[illegible]		[illegible]	.	[illegible]	[illegible]
[illegible]	[illegible]		[illegible]	.	[illegible]	[illegible]
Total,	[illegible]	.	[illegible]	[illegible]	[illegible]	[illegible]

and Result of the Causes Tried or otherwise disposed of on Circuit in the Year 1895, by Judges' Registrars.

Verdict for Plaintiff subject to Special Case	Verdict by Consent with Reference	Nonsuit	Verdict for Defendant	Jury discharged without Verdict	Juror withdrawn	Rule Nisi	NATURE OF THE ACTIONS ENTERED FOR TRIAL AND DISPOSED OF AS IN THIS RETURN.
..	..	..	..	..	..	..	On Negotiable Instruments, Bills of Exchange, &c.
..	..	..	..	5	..	..	On Bonds.
..	..	..	6	..	..	..	For Goods sold and delivered.
..	..	..	5	4	..	..	For Work and Labour done.
..	..	..	3	2	..	..	For Money lent, advanced, or paid.
..	3	..	2	..	..	..	For Money received.
..	..	..	..	..	..	..	For Compensation for Personal Injuries and Compensation under Lord Campbell's Act.
..	..	..	..	..	..	..	Against Carriers for Negligence.
..	..	..	1	1	..	..	Against Professional Men for Negligence.
..	..	..	4	..	..	..	For Compensation for other Injuries from Negligence.
..	..	..	8	..	..	..	Actions in the nature of Actions of Trover or Detinue.
..	1	..	3	..	..	..	For Breach of Contract.
..	..	..	..	..	..	..	For Breach of Warranty.
..	..	..	2	..	..	..	For Recovery of Land (Ejectment).
..	1	..	..	3	..	..	Trespass relative to Land, Houses, &c.
..	..	..	1	..	..	..	For Breach of Promise of Marriage.
..	..	..	..	..	..	..	Seduction.
..	..	..	1	..	..	..	Libel.
..	1	..	6	..	..	..	Slander.
..	..	..	..	..	..	..	Malicious Prosecution.
..	..	..	4	..	..	..	Assault.
..	2	..	1	..	..	..	False Imprisonment.
..	..	..	1	..	..	..	Issues from Courts of Equity.
..	..	..	1	..	..	..	For Breach of Covenant.
..	..	..	2	..	..	..	For Recovery of Rent.
..	..	..	2	..	..	..	Rights of Way.
..	..	..	..	1	..	..	Probate of Will.
..	..	..	..	..	..	..	Dower.
..	..	..	..	..	..	..	Wrongful Dismissal.
..	1	..	..	..	..	..	Compensation and Publication in Writs.
..	..	..	..	..	..	..	Mesne Rates.
..	6	..	48	10	..	..	Total.

TABLE 48.—HIGH COURT OF JUSTICE.—PROCEEDINGS ON CIRCUIT.—Nature of
in the Year 1898, from Returns

NATURE OF THE ACTIONS	[illegible]	NUMBER OF EACH CLASS OF						
		[illegible]	[illegible]	[illegible]	[illegible]	[illegible]	[illegible]	[illegible]
On Promissory Notes, Bills of Exchange, &c.	[illegible]	.		.		.		.
On Bonds,	[illegible]	.	.	.		.	.	.
For Goods sold and delivered,	[illegible]	.	.	.	.	.	.	.
For Work and Labour done,	[illegible]	.	.	.	.	.	.	.
For Money paid, advanced, or lent,	[illegible]	.	.	.	.	.	.	[illegible]
For Money received,	[illegible]	.	.	.	.	.	[illegible]	.
For Compensation for Personal Injuries and Compensation under Lord Campbell's Act,	[illegible]	.	.	.	.	.	.	.
Actions Chiefly for Negligence,	.	.	.	.	.	.	.	.
Against Professional Men for Negligence,	.	.	.	.	.	.	.	.
For Compensation for other Injuries from Negligence,	[illegible]	.	.	.	.	.	.	.
Actions in the nature of Actions of Trover or Detinue,	[illegible]	.	.	.	.	.	.	.
For Breach of Contract,	[illegible]	.	.	.	.	.	[illegible]	.
For Breach of Warranty,	[illegible]	.	.	.	.	.	.	.
For Recovery of Land (Ejectment),	[illegible]	.	.	.	.	.	.	.
Trespass relative to Land, Houses, &c.	[illegible]	.	.	.	.	.	.	.
For Breach of Promise of Marriage,	[illegible]	.	.	.	.	.	.	.
Seduction,	[illegible]	.	.	.	.	.	.	.
Libel,	[illegible]	.	.	.	.	.	.	.
Slander,	1	.	.	.	.	.	.	.
Malicious Prosecution,	[illegible]	.	.	.	.	.	.	.
Assault,	[illegible]	.	.	.	.	.	.	.
Interpleader Issues,	.	.	.	.	.	.	.	.
Issues from Courts of Equity,	.	.	.	.	.	.	.	.
For Breach of Covenant,	[illegible]	.	.	.	.	.	.	.
For Recovery of Rent,	.	.	.	.	.	.	.	.
Right of Way,	.	.	.	.	.	.	.	.
Probate of Will,	[illegible]	.	.	.	.	.	.	.
Divorce,	[illegible]	.	.	.	.	.	.	.
Wrongful Dismissal,	[illegible]	.	.	.	.	.	.	.
Obstruction and Pollution of Water,	[illegible]	.	.	.	.	.	.	.
Hence Rates,	[illegible]	.	.	.	.	.	.	.
TOTAL,	77	.	.	.	.	.	[illegible]	1

the Causes Tried on Circuit, the Classes of Amounts, and the Total Amount recovered, made by Judges' Registrars.

Amounts Recovered on Verdict.				Verdicts for Defendants [illegible]		Total Amount Recovered.	Nature of the Actions.
[illegible]	[illegible]	[illegible]	[illegible]	[illegible]	[illegible]	£ s. d.	
[illegible]	[illegible]	[illegible]	[illegible]	[illegible]	[illegible]	4 0 0	On Promissory Notes, Bills of Exchange, &c.
[illegible]	[illegible]	[illegible]	[illegible]	[illegible]	[illegible]	49 5 4	On Bonds.
[illegible]	[illegible]	[illegible]	[illegible]	[illegible]	[illegible]	[illegible]	For Goods sold and delivered.
[illegible]	[illegible]	[illegible]	[illegible]	[illegible]	[illegible]	[illegible]	For Work and Labour done.
[illegible]	[illegible]	[illegible]	[illegible]	[illegible]	[illegible]	[illegible]	For Money paid, advanced, or lent.
[illegible]	[illegible]	[illegible]	[illegible]	[illegible]	[illegible]	[illegible]	For Money received.
[illegible]	[illegible]	[illegible]	[illegible]	[illegible]	[illegible]	[illegible]	For Compensation for Personal Injuries and Compensation under Lord Campbell's Act.
[illegible]	[illegible]	[illegible]	[illegible]	[illegible]	[illegible]	—	Against Carriers for Negligence.
[illegible]	[illegible]	[illegible]	[illegible]	[illegible]	[illegible]	—	Against Professional Men for Negligence.
[illegible]	[illegible]	[illegible]	[illegible]	[illegible]	[illegible]	[illegible]	For Compensation for other Injuries from Negligence.
[illegible]	[illegible]	[illegible]	[illegible]	[illegible]	[illegible]	—	Actions in the nature of Actions of Trover or Detinue.
[illegible]	[illegible]	[illegible]	[illegible]	[illegible]	[illegible]	[illegible]	For Breach of Promise.
[illegible]	[illegible]	[illegible]	[illegible]	[illegible]	[illegible]	[illegible]	For Breach of Warranty.
[illegible]	[illegible]	[illegible]	[illegible]	[illegible]	[illegible]	[illegible]	For Recovery of Land (Ejectment).
[illegible]	[illegible]	[illegible]	[illegible]	[illegible]	[illegible]	[illegible]	Trespass relating to Land, Houses, &c.
[illegible]	[illegible]	[illegible]	[illegible]	[illegible]	[illegible]	[illegible]	For Breach of Promise of Marriage.
[illegible]	[illegible]	[illegible]	[illegible]	[illegible]	[illegible]	[illegible]	Seduction.
[illegible]	[illegible]	[illegible]	[illegible]	[illegible]	[illegible]	[illegible]	Libel.
[illegible]	[illegible]	[illegible]	[illegible]	[illegible]	[illegible]	[illegible]	Slander.
[illegible]	[illegible]	[illegible]	[illegible]	[illegible]	[illegible]	[illegible]	Malicious Prosecution.
[illegible]	[illegible]	[illegible]	[illegible]	[illegible]	[illegible]	[illegible]	Assault.
[illegible]	[illegible]	[illegible]	[illegible]	[illegible]	[illegible]	—	Interpleader Issues.
[illegible]	[illegible]	[illegible]	[illegible]	[illegible]	[illegible]	—	Issues from Courts of Equity.
[illegible]	[illegible]	[illegible]	[illegible]	[illegible]	[illegible]	[illegible]	For Breach of Covenant.
[illegible]	[illegible]	[illegible]	[illegible]	[illegible]	[illegible]	—	For Recovery of Rent.
[illegible]	[illegible]	[illegible]	[illegible]	[illegible]	[illegible]	—	Right of Way.
[illegible]	[illegible]	[illegible]	[illegible]	[illegible]	[illegible]	—	Probate of Will.
[illegible]	[illegible]	[illegible]	[illegible]	[illegible]	[illegible]	—	Divorce.
[illegible]	[illegible]	[illegible]	[illegible]	[illegible]	[illegible]	[illegible]	Wrongful Dismissal.
[illegible]	[illegible]	[illegible]	[illegible]	[illegible]	[illegible]	[illegible]	Obstruction and Pollution of Water.
[illegible]	[illegible]	[illegible]	[illegible]	[illegible]	[illegible]	[illegible]	Mines [illegible].
5	14	[illegible]	[illegible]	1	1	[illegible]	Total.

TABLE 49.—HIGH COURT OF JUSTICE.—PROCEEDINGS ON CIRCUIT.—Non-Attendance as Jurors, and Fiscal Presentments, from

Counties and Counties of Cities and Towns, arranged in Circuits.	[illegible]						[illegible]					
	Spring Assizes.			Summer Assizes.			Spring Assizes.			Summer Assizes.		
	Number.	Amounts claimed in cases where verdicts were given.	Amount found by verdicts.	Number.	Amounts claimed in cases where verdicts were given.	Amount found by verdicts.	Number.	Amounts claimed in cases where verdicts were given.	Amount found by verdicts.	Number.	Amounts claimed in cases where verdicts were given.	Amount found by verdicts.
LEINSTER CIRCUIT:		£ s. d.	£ s. d.		£ s. d.	£ s. d.		£ s. d.	£ s. d.		£ s. d.	£ s. d.
Carlow,	.	—	—	.	—	—	.	—	—	.	—	—
Kildare,	.	—	—	.	—	—	.	—	—	.	—	—
Kilkenny,	.	—	—	.	—	—	.	—	—	.	—	—
Kilkenny City,	.	—	—	.	—	—	.	—	—	.	—	—
Queen's County,	.	—	—	.	—	—	.	—	—	.	—	—
Tipperary, N.R.,	.	—	—	.	—	—	.	—	—	.	—	—
Tipperary, S.R.,	.	—	—	.	—	—	.	—	—	.	—	—
Waterford County,	.	—	—	.	—	—	.	—	—	.	—	—
Waterford City,	.	—	—	.	—	—	.	—	—	.	—	—
Wexford,	.	—	—	.	—	—	.	—	—	.	—	—
Wicklow,	.	—	—	.	—	—	.	—	—	.	—	—
MUNSTER CIRCUIT:												
Clare,	.	—	—	.	—	—	.	—	—	.	—	—
Cork County,	.	—	—	.	—	—	.	—	—	.	—	—
Cork City,	.	—	—	.	—	—	.	—	—	.	—	—
Kerry,	.	—	—	.	—	—	.	—	—	.	—	—
Limerick County,	.	—	—	.	—	—	.	—	—	.	—	—
Limerick City,	.	—	—	.	—	—	.	—	—	.	—	—
NORTH-EAST CIRCUIT:												
Antrim,	.	—	—	.	—	—	.	—	—	.	—	—
Armagh,	.	—	—	.	—	—	.	—	—	.	—	—
Carrickfergus Town,	.	—	—	.	—	—	.	—	—	.	—	—
Down,	.	—	—	[illegible]	[illegible] 0 0	[illegible] 0 0	.	—	—	.	—	—
Drogheda Town,	.	—	—	.	—	—	.	—	—	.	—	—
Louth,	.	—	—	.	—	—	.	—	—	.	—	—
Meath,	.	—	—	.	—	—	.	—	—	.	—	—
Monaghan,	.	—	—	.	—	—	.	—	—	.	—	—
NORTH-WEST CIRCUIT:												
Cavan,	.	—	—	.	—	—	.	—	—	.	—	—
Donegal,	.	—	—	.	—	—	.	—	—	.	—	—
Fermanagh,	.	—	—	.	—	—	.	—	—	.	—	—
Londonderry,	.	—	—	.	—	—	.	—	—	.	—	—
Longford,	.	—	—	.	—	—	.	—	—	.	—	—
Tyrone,	.	—	—	.	—	—	.	—	—	.	—	—
Westmeath,	.	—	—	.	—	—	.	—	—	.	—	—
CONNAUGHT CIRCUIT:												
Galway County,	.	—	—	.	—	—	.	—	—	.	—	—
Galway Town,	.	—	—	.	—	—	.	—	—	.	—	—
King's County,	.	—	—	.	—	—	.	—	—	.	—	—
Leitrim,	.	—	—	.	—	—	.	—	—	.	—	—
Mayo,	.	—	—	.	—	—	.	—	—	.	—	—
Roscommon,	.	—	—	.	—	—	.	—	—	.	—	—
Sligo,	.	—	—	.	—	—	.	—	—	.	—	—
TOTAL,	.	—	—	[illegible]	[illegible] 0 0	[illegible] 0 0	.	—	—	.	—	—

Proceedings in regard to Traverses, and Appeals from Persons Fined for Returns made by Clerks of the Crown, for the Year 18[illegible].

[illegible]	Spring Assizes.		[illegible]	Summer Assizes.		Number.			[illegible]	[illegible]	[illegible]	[illegible]	Counties and Counties of Cities and Towns, arranged in Circuits.
	£ s. d.	£ s. d.		£ s. d.	£ s. d.				£ s. d.	£ s. d.			Leinster Circuit:
	—	—		—	—				—	—			Carlow.
	—	—		—	—	[illegible]	[illegible]		[illegible]	—			Kildare.
	—	—		—	—				—	—			Kilkenny.
	—	—		—	—				—	—			Kilkenny City.
	—	—		—	—				—	—			Queen's County.
	—	—		—	—				—	—			Tipperary, N.R.
	—	—		—	—				—	—	[illegible]	[illegible]	Tipperary, S.R.
	—	—		—	—				—	—	[illegible]	[illegible]	Waterford County.
	—	—	[illegible]	[illegible]	[illegible]				—	—			Waterford City.
[illegible]	—	—	[illegible]	—	—	[illegible]	[illegible]		[illegible]	—			Wexford.
	—	—		—	—	[illegible]	[illegible]		[illegible]	—			Wicklow.
													Munster Circuit:
	—	—		—	—				—	—			Clare.
[illegible]	[illegible]	[illegible]	[illegible]	[illegible]	[illegible]	[illegible]	[illegible]		[illegible]	[illegible]			Cork County.
	—	—		—	—				—	—			Cork City.
[illegible]	—	—		—	—	[illegible]		[illegible]	—	—			Kerry.
	—	—	[illegible]	[illegible]	[illegible]				—	—			Limerick County.
	—	—		—	—				—	—			Limerick City.
													North-East Circuit:
[illegible]	[illegible]	[illegible]	[illegible]	[illegible]	[illegible]	[illegible]	[illegible]		[illegible]	—			Antrim.
	—	—		—	—				—	—		[illegible]	Armagh.
[illegible]	—	—		—	—				—	—			Carrickfergus Town.
	—	—	[illegible]	[illegible]	[illegible]				—	—		[illegible]	Down.
	—	—		—	—				—	—			Drogheda Town.
[illegible]	[illegible]	[illegible]		—	—				—	—			Louth.
	—	—		—	—				—	—		[illegible]	Meath.
	—	—		—	—				—	—			Monaghan.
													North-West Circuit:
	—	—		—	—	[illegible]	[illegible]		[illegible]	—		[illegible]	Cavan.
[illegible]	[illegible]	[illegible]	[illegible]	[illegible]	[illegible]				—	—			Donegal.
	—	—	[illegible]	[illegible]	[illegible]				—	—			Fermanagh.
[illegible]	[illegible]	[illegible]		—	—	[illegible]	[illegible]		[illegible]	—			Londonderry.
[illegible]	[illegible]	[illegible]	[illegible]	[illegible]	[illegible]				—	—			Longford.
	—	—		—	—				—	—			Tyrone.
	—	—		—	—				—	—			Westmeath.
													Connaught Circuit:
	—	—		—	—				—	—			Galway County.
	—	—		—	—				—	—			Galway Town.
	—	—		—	—				—	—			King's County.
	—	—		—	—				—	—			Leitrim.
	—	—		—	—				—	—			Mayo.
	—	—		—	—				—	—		[illegible]	Roscommon.
	—	—		—	—				—	—			Sligo.
[illegible]	[illegible]	[illegible]	[illegible]	[illegible]	[illegible]	[illegible]	[illegible]	1	[illegible]	[illegible]	[illegible]	[illegible]	Total.

* Where no amount appears in this column it signifies that the fines were altogether remitted.

TABLE 50.—HIGH COURT OF JUSTICE.—PROCEEDINGS ON CIRCUIT.—Appeals from County Court Judges and Recorders in 1896, from Returns made by Clerks of the Peace and Registrars of Recorders.

Counties and Counties of Cities and of Towns arranged in Circuits.	Appeals from County Court Judges and Recorders.			
	Entered.	Heard.		Struck Out, Withdrawn, Settled, &c.
		Affirmed.	Varied or Reversed.	
Leinster Circuit:				
Carlow,	[illegible]	[illegible]	[illegible]	[illegible]
Kildare,	[illegible]	[illegible]	[illegible]	[illegible]
Kilkenny,	[illegible]	[illegible]	[illegible]	[illegible]
Queen's County,	[illegible]	[illegible]	[illegible]	[illegible]
Tipperary, North Riding, / Tipperary, South Riding,	[illegible]	[illegible]	[illegible]	[illegible]
Waterford,	[illegible]	[illegible]	6	[illegible]
Wexford,	[illegible]	[illegible]	[illegible]	[illegible]
Wicklow,	[illegible]	[illegible]	[illegible]	[illegible]
Total,	[illegible]	[illegible]	[illegible]	[illegible]

TABLE 51.—COUNTY COURTS AND RECORDERS' COURTS.—Civil Bill Ejectments, Replevins, and other Civil Bills Served by Civil Bill Officers in 1866, from Returns made by Civil Bill Officers appointed by County Court Judges and Recorders.

[illegible]	[illegible]	[illegible]	[illegible]	[illegible]		
				Civil Bill Ejectments	Replevins	Other Civil Bills
Leinster.						
Carlow,	[illegible]	[illegible]	..	[illegible]	[illegible]	[illegible]
Dublin,	[illegible]	[illegible]	..	[illegible]	[illegible]	[illegible]
Dublin City,	[illegible]	[illegible]		[illegible]	..	[illegible]
Kildare,	[illegible]	[illegible]	..	[illegible]	[illegible]	[illegible]
Kilkenny, and City,	[illegible]	[illegible]	..	[illegible]	..	[illegible]
King's County,	[illegible]	[illegible]	..	[illegible]	[illegible]	[illegible]
Longford,	[illegible]	[illegible]	..	[illegible]	[illegible]	[illegible]
Louth, and Drogheda Town,	[illegible]	[illegible]	..	[illegible]	..	[illegible]
Meath,	[illegible]	[illegible]	..	[illegible]	[illegible]	[illegible]
Queen's County,	[illegible]	[illegible]	..	[illegible]	[illegible]	[illegible]
Westmeath,	[illegible]	[illegible]	..	[illegible]	[illegible]	[illegible]
Wexford,	[illegible]	[illegible]	..	[illegible]	[illegible]	[illegible]
Wicklow,	[illegible]	[illegible]	..	[illegible]	..	[illegible]
Total of Leinster,	[illegible]	[illegible]	..	[illegible]	[illegible]	[illegible]
Munster.						
Clare,	[illegible]	[illegible]	..	[illegible]	[illegible]	[illegible]
Cork, East Riding,	[illegible]	[illegible]	..	[illegible]	[illegible]	[illegible]
Cork, West Riding,	[illegible]	[illegible]	..	[illegible]	[illegible]	[illegible]
Cork City (Recorder's Court),	[illegible]	[illegible]	..	[illegible]	[illegible]	[illegible]
Kerry,	[illegible]	[illegible]	..	[illegible]	[illegible]	[illegible]
Limerick, and City,	[illegible]	[illegible]	..	[illegible]	[illegible]	[illegible]
Tipperary,	[illegible]	[illegible]	..	[illegible]	[illegible]	[illegible]
Waterford, and City,	[illegible]	[illegible]	..	[illegible]	[illegible]	[illegible]
Total of Munster,	[illegible]	[illegible]	..	[illegible]	[illegible]	[illegible]
Ulster.						
Antrim (including Carrickfergus),	[illegible]	[illegible]	..	[illegible]	[illegible]	[illegible]
Armagh,	[illegible]	[illegible]	..	[illegible]	[illegible]	[illegible]
Cavan,	[illegible]	[illegible]	..	[illegible]	[illegible]	[illegible]
Donegal,	[illegible]	[illegible]	..	[illegible]	[illegible]	[illegible]
Down,	[illegible]	[illegible]	..	[illegible]	[illegible]	[illegible]
Fermanagh,	[illegible]	[illegible]	..	[illegible]	[illegible]	[illegible]
Londonderry,	[illegible]	[illegible]	..	[illegible]	[illegible]	[illegible]
Monaghan,	[illegible]	[illegible]	..	[illegible]	[illegible]	[illegible]
Tyrone,	[illegible]	[illegible]	..	[illegible]	[illegible]	[illegible]
Total of Ulster,	[illegible]	[illegible]	..	[illegible]	[illegible]	[illegible]
Connaught.						
Galway, and Town,	[illegible]	[illegible]	..	[illegible]	[illegible]	[illegible]
Leitrim,	[illegible]	[illegible]	..	[illegible]	[illegible]	[illegible]
Mayo,	[illegible]	[illegible]	..	[illegible]	[illegible]	[illegible]
Roscommon,	[illegible]	[illegible]	..	[illegible]	[illegible]	[illegible]
Sligo,	[illegible]	[illegible]	..	[illegible]	[illegible]	[illegible]
Total of Connaught,	[illegible]	[illegible]	..	[illegible]	[illegible]	[illegible]
Total of Ireland,	[illegible]	[illegible]	..	[illegible]	[illegible]	[illegible]

TABLE 52.—COUNTY COURTS AND
Jurisdiction

all Suits (except at Land Sessions, Equity Sessions, and under Local Admiralty by Clerks of the Peace and Registrars of Recorders.

[illegible]	[illegible]	[illegible]	[illegible]	[illegible]	[illegible]	[illegible]	[illegible]	[illegible]	[illegible]	[illegible]	[illegible]	[illegible]	[illegible]	[illegible]	[illegible]	COUNTIES
																LEINSTER:
[illegible]	[illegible]	[illegible]	[illegible]	[illegible]	[illegible]	[illegible]	[illegible]	[illegible]	[illegible]	[illegible]	[illegible]	[illegible]	[illegible]	[illegible]	[illegible]	Carlow.
[illegible]	[illegible]	[illegible]	[illegible]	[illegible]	[illegible]	[illegible]	[illegible]	[illegible]	[illegible]	[illegible]	[illegible]	[illegible]	[illegible]	[illegible]	[illegible]	Dublin.
[illegible]	[illegible]	[illegible]	[illegible]	[illegible]	[illegible]	[illegible]	[illegible]	[illegible]	[illegible]	[illegible]	[illegible]	[illegible]	[illegible]	[illegible]	[illegible]	Dublin City (Recorder's Court).
[illegible]	[illegible]	[illegible]	[illegible]	[illegible]	[illegible]	[illegible]	[illegible]	[illegible]	[illegible]	[illegible]	[illegible]	[illegible]	[illegible]	[illegible]	[illegible]	Kildare.
[illegible]	[illegible]	[illegible]	[illegible]	[illegible]	[illegible]	[illegible]	[illegible]	[illegible]	[illegible]	[illegible]	[illegible]	[illegible]	[illegible]	[illegible]	[illegible]	Kilkenny.
[illegible]	[illegible]	[illegible]	[illegible]	[illegible]	[illegible]	[illegible]	[illegible]	[illegible]	[illegible]	[illegible]	[illegible]	[illegible]	[illegible]	[illegible]	[illegible]	King's County.
[illegible]	[illegible]	[illegible]	[illegible]	[illegible]	[illegible]	[illegible]	[illegible]	[illegible]	[illegible]	[illegible]	[illegible]	[illegible]	[illegible]	[illegible]	[illegible]	Longford.
[illegible]	[illegible]	[illegible]	[illegible]	[illegible]	[illegible]	[illegible]	[illegible]	[illegible]	[illegible]	[illegible]	[illegible]	[illegible]	[illegible]	[illegible]	[illegible]	Louth.
[illegible]	[illegible]	[illegible]	[illegible]	[illegible]	[illegible]	[illegible]	[illegible]	[illegible]	[illegible]	[illegible]	[illegible]	[illegible]	[illegible]	[illegible]	[illegible]	Meath.
[illegible]	[illegible]	[illegible]	[illegible]	[illegible]	[illegible]	[illegible]	[illegible]	[illegible]	[illegible]	[illegible]	[illegible]	[illegible]	[illegible]	[illegible]	[illegible]	Queen's County.
[illegible]	[illegible]	[illegible]	[illegible]	[illegible]	[illegible]	[illegible]	[illegible]	[illegible]	[illegible]	[illegible]	[illegible]	[illegible]	[illegible]	[illegible]	[illegible]	Westmeath.
[illegible]	[illegible]	[illegible]	[illegible]	[illegible]	[illegible]	[illegible]	[illegible]	[illegible]	[illegible]	[illegible]	[illegible]	[illegible]	[illegible]	[illegible]	[illegible]	Wexford.
[illegible]	[illegible]	[illegible]	[illegible]	[illegible]	[illegible]	[illegible]	[illegible]	[illegible]	[illegible]	[illegible]	[illegible]	[illegible]	[illegible]	[illegible]	[illegible]	Wicklow.
[illegible]	[illegible]	[illegible]	[illegible]	[illegible]	[illegible]	[illegible]	[illegible]	[illegible]	[illegible]	[illegible]	[illegible]	[illegible]	[illegible]	[illegible]	[illegible]	Total of Leinster.
																MUNSTER:
[illegible]	[illegible]	[illegible]	[illegible]	[illegible]	[illegible]	[illegible]	[illegible]	[illegible]	[illegible]	[illegible]	[illegible]	[illegible]	[illegible]	[illegible]	[illegible]	Clare.
[illegible]	[illegible]	[illegible]	[illegible]	[illegible]	[illegible]	[illegible]	[illegible]	[illegible]	[illegible]	[illegible]	[illegible]	[illegible]	[illegible]	[illegible]	[illegible]	Cork, E.R.
[illegible]	[illegible]	[illegible]	[illegible]	[illegible]	[illegible]	[illegible]	[illegible]	[illegible]	[illegible]	[illegible]	[illegible]	[illegible]	[illegible]	[illegible]	[illegible]	Cork, W.R.
[illegible]	[illegible]	[illegible]	[illegible]	[illegible]	[illegible]	[illegible]	[illegible]	[illegible]	[illegible]	[illegible]	[illegible]	[illegible]	[illegible]	[illegible]	[illegible]	Cork City (Recorder's Court).
[illegible]	[illegible]	[illegible]	[illegible]	[illegible]	[illegible]	[illegible]	[illegible]	[illegible]	[illegible]	[illegible]	[illegible]	[illegible]	[illegible]	[illegible]	[illegible]	Kerry.
[illegible]	[illegible]	[illegible]	[illegible]	[illegible]	[illegible]	[illegible]	[illegible]	[illegible]	[illegible]	[illegible]	[illegible]	[illegible]	[illegible]	[illegible]	[illegible]	Limerick.
[illegible]	[illegible]	[illegible]	[illegible]	[illegible]	[illegible]	[illegible]	[illegible]	[illegible]	[illegible]	[illegible]	[illegible]	[illegible]	[illegible]	[illegible]	[illegible]	Tipperary.
[illegible]	[illegible]	[illegible]	[illegible]	[illegible]	[illegible]	[illegible]	[illegible]	[illegible]	[illegible]	[illegible]	[illegible]	[illegible]	[illegible]	[illegible]	[illegible]	Waterford.
[illegible]	[illegible]	[illegible]	[illegible]	[illegible]	[illegible]	[illegible]	[illegible]	[illegible]	[illegible]	[illegible]	[illegible]	[illegible]	[illegible]	[illegible]	[illegible]	Total of Munster.
																ULSTER:
[illegible]	[illegible]	[illegible]	[illegible]	[illegible]	[illegible]	[illegible]	[illegible]	[illegible]	[illegible]	[illegible]	[illegible]	[illegible]	[illegible]	[illegible]	[illegible]	Antrim.
[illegible]	[illegible]	[illegible]	[illegible]	[illegible]	[illegible]	[illegible]	[illegible]	[illegible]	[illegible]	[illegible]	[illegible]	[illegible]	[illegible]	[illegible]	[illegible]	Armagh.
[illegible]	[illegible]	[illegible]	[illegible]	[illegible]	[illegible]	[illegible]	[illegible]	[illegible]	[illegible]	[illegible]	[illegible]	[illegible]	[illegible]	[illegible]	[illegible]	Belfast (Recorder's Court).
[illegible]	[illegible]	[illegible]	[illegible]	[illegible]	[illegible]	[illegible]	[illegible]	[illegible]	[illegible]	[illegible]	[illegible]	[illegible]	[illegible]	[illegible]	[illegible]	Cavan.
[illegible]	[illegible]	[illegible]	[illegible]	[illegible]	[illegible]	[illegible]	[illegible]	[illegible]	[illegible]	[illegible]	[illegible]	[illegible]	[illegible]	[illegible]	[illegible]	Donegal.
[illegible]	[illegible]	[illegible]	[illegible]	[illegible]	[illegible]	[illegible]	[illegible]	[illegible]	[illegible]	[illegible]	[illegible]	[illegible]	[illegible]	[illegible]	[illegible]	Down.
[illegible]	[illegible]	[illegible]	[illegible]	[illegible]	[illegible]	[illegible]	[illegible]	[illegible]	[illegible]	[illegible]	[illegible]	[illegible]	[illegible]	[illegible]	[illegible]	Fermanagh.
[illegible]	[illegible]	[illegible]	[illegible]	[illegible]	[illegible]	[illegible]	[illegible]	[illegible]	[illegible]	[illegible]	[illegible]	[illegible]	[illegible]	[illegible]	[illegible]	Londonderry.
[illegible]	[illegible]	[illegible]	[illegible]	[illegible]	[illegible]	[illegible]	[illegible]	[illegible]	[illegible]	[illegible]	[illegible]	[illegible]	[illegible]	[illegible]	[illegible]	Londonderry City (Recorder's Court).
[illegible]	[illegible]	[illegible]	[illegible]	[illegible]	[illegible]	[illegible]	[illegible]	[illegible]	[illegible]	[illegible]	[illegible]	[illegible]	[illegible]	[illegible]	[illegible]	Monaghan.
[illegible]	[illegible]	[illegible]	[illegible]	[illegible]	[illegible]	[illegible]	[illegible]	[illegible]	[illegible]	[illegible]	[illegible]	[illegible]	[illegible]	[illegible]	[illegible]	Tyrone.
[illegible]	[illegible]	[illegible]	[illegible]	[illegible]	[illegible]	[illegible]	[illegible]	[illegible]	[illegible]	[illegible]	[illegible]	[illegible]	[illegible]	[illegible]	[illegible]	Total of Ulster.
																CONNAUGHT:
[illegible]	[illegible]	[illegible]	[illegible]	[illegible]	[illegible]	[illegible]	[illegible]	[illegible]	[illegible]	[illegible]	[illegible]	[illegible]	[illegible]	[illegible]	[illegible]	Galway.
[illegible]	[illegible]	[illegible]	[illegible]	[illegible]	[illegible]	[illegible]	[illegible]	[illegible]	[illegible]	[illegible]	[illegible]	[illegible]	[illegible]	[illegible]	[illegible]	Galway Town (Recorder's Court).
[illegible]	[illegible]	[illegible]	[illegible]	[illegible]	[illegible]	[illegible]	[illegible]	[illegible]	[illegible]	[illegible]	[illegible]	[illegible]	[illegible]	[illegible]	[illegible]	Leitrim.
[illegible]	[illegible]	[illegible]	[illegible]	[illegible]	[illegible]	[illegible]	[illegible]	[illegible]	[illegible]	[illegible]	[illegible]	[illegible]	[illegible]	[illegible]	[illegible]	Mayo.
[illegible]	[illegible]	[illegible]	[illegible]	[illegible]	[illegible]	[illegible]	[illegible]	[illegible]	[illegible]	[illegible]	[illegible]	[illegible]	[illegible]	[illegible]	[illegible]	Roscommon.
[illegible]	[illegible]	[illegible]	[illegible]	[illegible]	[illegible]	[illegible]	[illegible]	[illegible]	[illegible]	[illegible]	[illegible]	[illegible]	[illegible]	[illegible]	[illegible]	Sligo.
[illegible]	[illegible]	[illegible]	[illegible]	[illegible]	[illegible]	[illegible]	[illegible]	[illegible]	[illegible]	[illegible]	[illegible]	[illegible]	[illegible]	[illegible]	[illegible]	Total of Connaught.
[illegible]	[illegible]	[illegible]	[illegible]	[illegible]	[illegible]	[illegible]	[illegible]	[illegible]	[illegible]	[illegible]	[illegible]	[illegible]	[illegible]	[illegible]	[illegible]	Total of Ireland.

TABLE 59.—COUNTY COURTS AND RECORDERS' COURTS.—Results of Equity Civil

COUNTIES.	[illegible]	[illegible]					[illegible]				[illegible]	
		Total.	[illegible]	[illegible]	[illegible]	[illegible]	TOTAL.	[illegible]	[illegible]	[illegible]	[illegible]	[illegible]
LEINSTER:												
Carlow,	[illegible]	[illegible]	[illegible]	.	.	.	.	.	.	.	.	.
Dublin,	[illegible]	[illegible]	[illegible]	.	.	[illegible]	[illegible]	[illegible]	[illegible]	.	.	[illegible]
Dublin City,	[illegible]	[illegible]	[illegible]	.	[illegible]	[illegible]	[illegible]	[illegible]	[illegible]	[illegible]	[illegible]	[illegible]
Kildare,	[illegible]	[illegible]	[illegible]	.	.	[illegible]	[illegible]	.	[illegible]	.	[illegible]	[illegible]
Kilkenny,	[illegible]	[illegible]	[illegible]	[illegible]	.	[illegible]	[illegible]	[illegible]	[illegible]	[illegible]	.	.
King's County,	[illegible]	[illegible]	[illegible]	.	.	[illegible]	[illegible]	[illegible]	.	.	.	.
Longford,	[illegible]	[illegible]	[illegible]	.	.	[illegible]	[illegible]	.	[illegible]	.	[illegible]	[illegible]
Louth,	[illegible]	[illegible]	[illegible]	.	.	[illegible]	.	.	.	.	.	.
Meath,	[illegible]	[illegible]	[illegible]	.	.	[illegible]	[illegible]	[illegible]	[illegible]	[illegible]	.	[illegible]
Queen's County,	[illegible]	[illegible]	[illegible]	.	.	[illegible]	[illegible]	.	[illegible]	.	.	.
Westmeath,	[illegible]	[illegible]	[illegible]	[illegible]	.	[illegible]	[illegible]	.	[illegible]	[illegible]	.	[illegible]
Wexford,	[illegible]	[illegible]	[illegible]	.	.	[illegible]	[illegible]	.	[illegible]	[illegible]	.	[illegible]
Wicklow,	[illegible]	[illegible]	[illegible]	.	.	[illegible]	[illegible]	.	[illegible]	.	.	.
Total,	[illegible]	[illegible]	[illegible]	[illegible]	[illegible]	[illegible]	[illegible]	[illegible]	[illegible]	[illegible]	[illegible]	[illegible]
MUNSTER:												
Clare,	[illegible]	[illegible]	[illegible]	.	.	[illegible]	.	.	.	.	.	.
Cork, East Riding,	[illegible]	[illegible]	[illegible]	.	[illegible]	[illegible]	[illegible]	[illegible]	[illegible]	.	.	.
Cork, West Riding,	[illegible]	[illegible]	[illegible]	[illegible]	.	[illegible]	[illegible]	.		[illegible]	[illegible]	[illegible]
Kerry,	[illegible]	[illegible]	[illegible]	[illegible]	.	[illegible]	[illegible]	[illegible]	[illegible]	.	[illegible]	[illegible]
Limerick,	[illegible]	[illegible]	[illegible]	[illegible]	.	[illegible]	[illegible]	[illegible]	[illegible]	.	.	.
Tipperary,	[illegible]	[illegible]	[illegible]	.	.	[illegible]	[illegible]	.	.	[illegible]	.	.
Waterford,	[illegible]	[illegible]	[illegible]	[illegible]	[illegible]	[illegible]	[illegible]	.	[illegible]	[illegible]	[illegible]	.
Total,	[illegible]	[illegible]	[illegible]	[illegible]	[illegible]	[illegible]	[illegible]	[illegible]	[illegible]	[illegible]	[illegible]	[illegible]
ULSTER:												
Antrim,	[illegible]	[illegible]	[illegible]	[illegible]	[illegible]	[illegible]	[illegible]	[illegible]	[illegible]	.	[illegible]	[illegible]
Armagh,	[illegible]	[illegible]	[illegible]	[illegible]	[illegible]	[illegible]	.	.	.	.	.	[illegible]
Cavan,	[illegible]	[illegible]	[illegible]	[illegible]	.	[illegible]	[illegible]	.	[illegible]	.	[illegible]	.
Donegal,	[illegible]	[illegible]	[illegible]	.	.	[illegible]	[illegible]	.	[illegible]	[illegible]	.	[illegible]
Down,	[illegible]	[illegible]	[illegible]	.	.	[illegible]	[illegible]	[illegible]	[illegible]	.	[illegible]	[illegible]
Fermanagh,	[illegible]	[illegible]	[illegible]	.	.	[illegible]	[illegible]	[illegible]	.	.	.	.
Londonderry,	[illegible]	[illegible]	[illegible]	[illegible]	.	[illegible]	[illegible]	.	[illegible]	[illegible]	.	[illegible]
Monaghan,	[illegible]	[illegible]	[illegible]	[illegible]		[illegible]	[illegible]	[illegible]	[illegible]	.	[illegible]	[illegible]
Tyrone,	[illegible]	[illegible]	[illegible]	.	.	[illegible]	.	.	.	.	.	[illegible]
Total,	[illegible]	[illegible]	[illegible]	[illegible]	[illegible]	[illegible]	[illegible]	[illegible]	[illegible]	[illegible]	[illegible]	[illegible]
CONNAUGHT:												
Galway,	[illegible]	[illegible]	[illegible]	.	[illegible]	[illegible]	[illegible]	[illegible]	[illegible]	.	.	.
Leitrim,	[illegible]	[illegible]	[illegible]	[illegible]	.	[illegible]	[illegible]	.	[illegible]	.	.	.
Mayo,	[illegible]	[illegible]	[illegible]	[illegible]	[illegible]	[illegible]	.	.	.	.	[illegible]	.
Roscommon,	[illegible]	[illegible]	[illegible]	[illegible]	.	.	[illegible]	[illegible]	[illegible]	[illegible]	.	.
Sligo,	[illegible]	[illegible]	[illegible]	[illegible]	.	[illegible]	[illegible]	[illegible]	[illegible]	[illegible]	[illegible]	[illegible]
Total,	[illegible]	[illegible]	[illegible]	[illegible]	[illegible]	[illegible]	[illegible]	[illegible]	[illegible]	[illegible]	[illegible]	[illegible]
TOTAL OF IRELAND,	[illegible]	[illegible]	[illegible]	[illegible]	[illegible]	[illegible]	[illegible]	[illegible]	[illegible]	[illegible]	[illegible]	[illegible]

Bills or Proceedings in the Year 1856, from Returns made by the Clerks of the Peace.

[illegible]	[illegible]	[illegible]	[illegible]	[illegible]	[illegible]	[illegible]	Number of Appeals	[illegible]	[illegible]	[illegible]	COUNTIES.
	£ s. d.			£ s. d.	£ s. d.						LEINSTER.
.	[illegible]	[illegible]	.	[illegible]	[illegible]	[illegible]	.	.	.	.	Carlow.
.	[illegible]	1	[illegible]	[illegible]	[illegible]	[illegible]	.	.	.	.	Dublin.
[illegible]	[illegible]	[illegible]	[illegible]	[illegible]	[illegible]	[illegible]	[illegible]	1	1	.	Dublin City.
.	.	[illegible]	[illegible]	[illegible]	[illegible]	[illegible]	[illegible]	.	.	.	Kildare.
.	[illegible]	[illegible]	.	[illegible]	[illegible]	[illegible]	.	.	.	.	Kilkenny.
.	[illegible]	.	.	[illegible]	[illegible]	[illegible]	.	.	.	.	King's County.
.	[illegible]	[illegible]	.	[illegible]	[illegible]	[illegible]	[illegible]	.	.	.	Longford.
.	[illegible]	[illegible]	.	[illegible]	[illegible]	[illegible]	.	.	.	.	Louth.
[illegible]	.	.	.	[illegible]	[illegible]	[illegible]	[illegible]	.	.	.	Meath.
.	.	[illegible]	.	[illegible]	[illegible]	.	.	.	.	.	Queen's County.
[illegible]	.	[illegible]	.	[illegible]	[illegible]	[illegible]	.	.	1	.	Westmeath.
.	.	[illegible]	.	[illegible]	[illegible]	[illegible]	.	.	.	.	Wexford.
.	[illegible]	.	.	[illegible]	[illegible]	[illegible]	.	.	.	.	Wicklow.
[illegible]	[illegible]	[illegible]	[illegible]	[illegible]	[illegible]	[illegible]	[illegible]	[illegible]	[illegible]	.	Total.
											MUNSTER.
.	.	[illegible]	.	[illegible]	[illegible]	[illegible]	[illegible]	.	.	.	Clare.
.	[illegible]	[illegible]	[illegible]	[illegible]	[illegible]	[illegible]	[illegible]	.	.	.	Cork, East Riding.
.	[illegible]	[illegible]	.	[illegible]	[illegible]	[illegible]	[illegible]	.	[illegible]	.	Cork, West Riding.
.	.	[illegible]	.	[illegible]	[illegible]	[illegible]	[illegible]	.	1	.	Kerry.
.	.	[illegible]	.	[illegible]	[illegible]	[illegible]	[illegible]	.	.	.	Limerick.
.	.	.	.	[illegible]	[illegible]	[illegible]	[illegible]	.	.	.	Tipperary.
.	.	[illegible]	.	[illegible]	[illegible]	[illegible]	.	.	.	.	Waterford.
.	[illegible]	[illegible]	[illegible]	[illegible]	[illegible]	[illegible]	[illegible]	.	[illegible]	.	Total.
											ULSTER:
.	[illegible]	[illegible]	[illegible]	[illegible]	[illegible]	[illegible]	[illegible]	.	.	.	Antrim.
[illegible]	[illegible]	[illegible]	.	[illegible]	[illegible]	[illegible]	[illegible]	.	.	.	Armagh.
.	[illegible]	[illegible]	.	[illegible]	[illegible]	[illegible]	[illegible]	.	1	.	Cavan.
[illegible]	[illegible]	[illegible]	.	[illegible]	[illegible]	[illegible]	[illegible]	.	1	.	Donegal.
.	[illegible]	.	[illegible]	[illegible]	[illegible]	[illegible]	[illegible]	.	[illegible]	.	Down.
.	.	.	.	[illegible]	[illegible]	.	[illegible]	.	.	.	Fermanagh.
.	[illegible]	[illegible]	.	[illegible]	[illegible]	[illegible]	[illegible]	.	[illegible]	.	Londonderry.
.	[illegible]	[illegible]	[illegible]	[illegible]	[illegible]	[illegible]	[illegible]	1	[illegible]	.	Monaghan.
.	[illegible]	[illegible]	.	[illegible]	[illegible]	[illegible]	[illegible]	.	.	.	Tyrone.
[illegible]	[illegible]	[illegible]	[illegible]	[illegible]	[illegible]	[illegible]	[illegible]	1	[illegible]	.	Total.
											CONNAUGHT:
[illegible]	[illegible]	[illegible]	[illegible]	[illegible]	[illegible]	[illegible]	[illegible]	.	.	.	Galway.
.	.	.	.	[illegible]	[illegible]	[illegible]	[illegible]	.	.	.	Leitrim.
[illegible]	[illegible]	[illegible]	.	[illegible]	[illegible]	[illegible]	[illegible]	.	.	.	Mayo.
.	.	[illegible]	.	[illegible]	[illegible]	[illegible]	[illegible]	.	.	.	Roscommon.
[illegible]	[illegible]	[illegible]	[illegible]	[illegible]	[illegible]	[illegible]	[illegible]	[illegible]	[illegible]	.	Sligo.
[illegible]	[illegible]	[illegible]	[illegible]	[illegible]	[illegible]	[illegible]	[illegible]	[illegible]	[illegible]	.	Total.
[illegible]	[illegible]	[illegible]	[illegible]	[illegible]	[illegible]	[illegible]	[illegible]	[illegible]	[illegible]	.	TOTAL OF IRELAND.

* Not ascertained.

TABLE 84.—COUNTY COURTS.—LAND SESSIONS.—Proceedings in the
Returns made by the

Counties, arranged by Provinces.	[illegible]	Land Sessions. Land Claim Cases.					Applications of Tenants to obtain Leases.				Applications of Tenants to register Improvements.				Appeals.			Result of Appeals.			
		[illegible]	[illegible]	[illegible]	[illegible]	[illegible]	[illegible]	[illegible]	[illegible]	[illegible]	[illegible]	[illegible]	[illegible]	[illegible]	[illegible]	[illegible]	[illegible]	[illegible]	[illegible]	[illegible]	[illegible]
Leinster:																					
Carlow,	-	-	-	-	-	-	-	-	-	-	-	-	-	-	-	-	-	-	-	-	-
Dublin,	-	-	-	-	-	-	-	-	-	-	-	-	-	-	-	-	-	-	-	-	-
Kildare,	[illegible]	[illegible]	[illegible]	-	-	-	-	-	-	-	-	-	-	-	-	-	-	-	-	-	-
Kilkenny,	-	-	-	-	-	-	-	-	-	-	-	-	-	-	-	-	-	-	-	-	-
King's County,	-	-	-	-	-	-	-	-	-	-	-	-	-	-	-	-	-	-	-	-	-
Longford,	-	-	-	-	-	-	-	-	-	-	-	-	-	-	-	-	-	-	-	-	-
Louth,	-	-	-	-	-	-	-	-	-	-	-	-	-	-	-	-	-	-	-	-	-
Meath,	-	-	-	-	-	-	-	-	-	-	-	-	-	-	-	-	-	-	-	-	-
Queen's County,	-	-	-	-	-	-	-	-	-	-	-	-	-	-	-	-	-	-	-	-	-
Westmeath,	-	-	-	-	-	-	-	-	-	-	-	-	-	-	-	-	-	-	-	-	-
Wexford,	[illegible]	[illegible]	[illegible]	[illegible]	-	-	-	-	-	-	-	-	-	-	-	-	-	-	-	-	-
Wicklow,	-	-	-	-	-	-	-	-	-	-	-	-	-	-	-	-	-	-	-	-	-
Total of Leinster,	[illegible]	[illegible]	[illegible]	[illegible]	-	-	-	-	-	-	-	-	-	-	-	-	-	-	-	-	-
Munster:																					
Clare,	[illegible]	[illegible]	[illegible]	-	[illegible]	-	-	-	-	-	-	-	-	-	-	-	-	-	-	-	-
Cork, E.R.,	-	-	-	-	-	-	-	-	-	-	-	-	-	-	-	-	-	-	-	-	-
Cork, W.R.,	-	-	-	-	-	-	-	-	-	-	-	-	-	-	-	-	-	-	-	-	-
Kerry,	-	-	-	-	-	-	-	-	-	-	-	-	-	-	-	-	-	-	-	-	-
Limerick,	-	-	-	-	-	-	-	-	-	-	-	-	-	-	-	-	-	-	-	-	-
Tipperary,	[illegible]	[illegible]	-	-	[illegible]	-	-	-	-	-	-	-	-	-	-	-	-	-	-	-	-
Waterford,	-	-	-	-	-	-	-	-	-	-	-	-	-	-	-	-	-	-	-	-	-
Total of Munster,	[illegible]	[illegible]	[illegible]	-	[illegible]	-	-	-	-	-	-	-	-	-	-	-	-	-	-	-	-
Ulster:																					
Antrim,	-	-	-	-	-	-	-	-	-	-	-	-	-	-	-	-	-	-	-	-	-
Armagh,	-	-	-	-	-	-	-	-	-	-	-	-	-	-	-	-	-	-	-	-	-
Cavan,	[illegible]	[illegible]	[illegible]	[illegible]	-	-	-	-	-	-	-	-	-	-	-	-	-	-	-	-	-
Donegal,	-	-	-	-	-	-	-	-	-	-	-	-	-	-	-	-	-	-	-	-	-
Down,	-	-	-	-	-	-	-	-	-	-	-	-	-	-	-	-	-	-	-	-	-
Fermanagh,	-	-	-	-	-	-	-	-	-	-	-	-	-	-	-	-	-	-	-	-	-
Londonderry,	-	-	-	-	-	-	-	-	-	-	-	-	-	-	-	-	-	-	-	-	-
Monaghan,	-	-	-	-	-	-	-	-	-	-	-	-	-	-	-	-	-	-	-	-	-
Tyrone,	-	-	-	-	-	-	-	-	-	-	-	-	-	-	-	-	-	-	-	-	-
Total of Ulster,	[illegible]	[illegible]	[illegible]	[illegible]	-	-	-	-	-	-	-	-	-	-	-	-	-	-	-	-	-
Connaught:																					
Galway,	-	-	-	-	-	-	-	-	-	-	-	-	-	-	-	-	-	-	-	-	-
Leitrim,	-	-	-	-	-	-	-	-	-	-	-	-	-	-	-	-	-	-	-	-	-
Mayo,	-	-	-	-	-	-	-	-	-	-	-	-	-	-	-	-	-	-	-	-	-
Roscommon,	-	-	-	-	-	-	-	-	-	-	-	-	-	-	-	-	-	-	-	-	-
Sligo,	-	-	-	-	-	-	-	-	-	-	-	-	-	-	-	-	-	-	-	-	-
Total of Connaught,	-	-	-	-	-	-	-	-	-	-	-	-	-	-	-	-	-	-	-	-	-
Total of Ireland,	[illegible]	[illegible]	[illegible]	[illegible]	[illegible]	-	-	-	-	-	-	-	-	-	-	-	-	-	-	-	-

Year 1898, under the Landlord and Tenant (Ireland) Act, 1870, from Clerks of the Peace.

Amount Claimed.					Amount Decreed, and Costs.					[illegible]						Counties arranged in Provinces.
[illegible]	[illegible]	[illegible]	[illegible]	[illegible]	[illegible]	[illegible]	[illegible]	[illegible]	[illegible]	Amount Claimed— [illegible]	[illegible]	[illegible]	[illegible]	[illegible]	[illegible]	
£	£	£	£	£	£	£	£	£	£	£	£	£	£	£	£	LEINSTER:
-	-	-	-	-	-	-	-	-	-	-	-	-	-	-	-	Carlow.
-	-	-	-	-	-	-	-	-	-	-	-	-	-	-	-	Dublin.
[illegible]	-	[illegible]	-	-	[illegible]	[illegible]	[illegible]	[illegible]	-	[illegible]	-	[illegible]	-	-	[illegible]	Kildare.
-	-	-	-	-	-	-	-	-	-	-	-	-	-	-	-	Kilkenny.
-	-	-	-	-	-	-	-	-	-	-	-	-	-	-	-	King's County.
-	-	-	-	-	-	-	-	-	-	-	-	-	-	-	-	Longford.
-	-	-	-	-	-	-	-	-	-	-	-	-	-	-	-	Louth.
-	-	-	-	-	-	-	-	-	-	-	-	-	-	-	-	Meath.
-	-	-	-	-	-	-	-	-	-	-	-	-	-	-	-	Queen's County.
-	-	-	-	-	-	-	-	-	-	-	-	-	-	-	-	Westmeath.
[illegible]	-	[illegible]	11	-	[illegible]	[illegible]	[illegible]	[illegible]	-	[illegible]	-	[illegible]	[illegible]	-	-	Wexford.
-	-	-	-	-	-	-	-	-	-	-	-	-	-	-	-	Wicklow.
[illegible]	-	[illegible]	11	-	[illegible]	[illegible]	[illegible]	[illegible]	-	[illegible]	-	[illegible]	11	-	[illegible]	Total of LEINSTER.
																MUNSTER:
[illegible]	[illegible]	[illegible]	-	-	[illegible]	-	[illegible]	[illegible]	-	[illegible]	[illegible]	[illegible]	-	-	[illegible]	Clare.
-	-	-	-	-	-	-	-	-	-	-	-	-	-	-	-	Cork, E.R.
-	-	-	-	-	-	-	-	-	-	-	-	-	-	-	-	Cork, W.R.
-	-	-	-	-	-	-	-	-	-	-	-	-	-	-	-	Kerry.
-	-	-	-	-	-	-	-	-	-	-	-	-	-	-	-	Limerick.
[illegible]	[illegible]	-	-	-	-	-	-	-	-	-	-	-	-	-	-	Tipperary.
-	-	-	-	-	-	-	-	-	-	-	-	-	-	-	-	Waterford.
[illegible]	[illegible]	[illegible]	-	-	[illegible]	-	[illegible]	[illegible]	-	[illegible]	[illegible]	[illegible]	-	-	[illegible]	Total of MUNSTER.
																ULSTER:
-	-	-	-	-	-	-	-	-	-	-	-	-	-	-	-	Antrim.
-	-	-	-	-	-	-	-	-	-	-	-	-	-	-	-	Armagh.
[illegible]	-	[illegible]	[illegible]	-	[illegible]	[illegible]	[illegible]	[illegible]	-	[illegible]	-	[illegible]	[illegible]	-	[illegible]	Cavan.
-	-	-	-	-	-	-	-	-	-	-	-	-	-	-	-	Donegal.
-	-	-	-	-	-	-	-	-	-	-	-	-	-	-	-	Down.
-	-	-	-	-	-	-	-	-	-	-	-	-	-	-	-	Fermanagh.
-	-	-	-	-	-	-	-	-	-	-	-	-	-	-	-	Londonderry.
-	-	-	-	-	-	-	-	-	-	-	-	-	-	-	-	Monaghan.
-	-	-	-	-	-	-	-	-	-	-	-	-	-	-	-	Tyrone.
[illegible]	-	[illegible]	[illegible]	-	[illegible]	[illegible]	[illegible]	[illegible]	-	[illegible]	-	[illegible]	[illegible]	-	[illegible]	Total of ULSTER.
																CONNAUGHT:
-	-	-	-	-	-	-	-	-	-	-	-	-	-	-	-	Galway.
-	-	-	-	-	-	-	-	-	-	-	-	-	-	-	-	Leitrim.
-	-	-	-	-	-	-	-	-	-	-	-	-	-	-	-	Mayo.
-	-	-	-	-	-	-	-	-	-	-	-	-	-	-	-	Roscommon.
-	-	-	-	-	-	-	-	-	-	-	-	-	-	-	-	Sligo.
-	-	-	-	-	-	-	-	-	-	-	-	-	-	-	-	Total of CONNAUGHT.
[illegible]	[illegible]	[illegible]	[illegible]	-	[illegible]	[illegible]	[illegible]	[illegible]	-	[illegible]	[illegible]	[illegible]	[illegible]	-	[illegible]	Total of IRELAND.

TABLE 54—[illegible]—COUNTY COURTS.—LAND SESSIONS.—Proceedings in the ... by the Clerks

COUNTIES, ARRANGED IN PROVINCES.	[illegible]						[illegible]						[illegible]					
	Amount Claimed.					[illegible]	Amount Claimed.					[illegible]	Amount Claimed.					[illegible]
	[illegible]	[illegible]	[illegible]	[illegible]	[illegible]	[illegible]	[illegible]	[illegible]	[illegible]	[illegible]	[illegible]	[illegible]	[illegible]	[illegible]	[illegible]	[illegible]	[illegible]	[illegible]
LEINSTER:	£	£	£	£	£	£	£	£	£	£	£	£	£	£	£	£	£	£
Carlow,	-	-	-	-	-	-	-	-	-	-	-	-	-	-	-	-	-	-
Dublin,	-	-	-	-	-	-	-	-	-	-	-	-	-	-	-	-	-	-
Kildare,	[illegible]	-	[illegible]	-	-	[illegible]	-	-	-	-	-	-	-	-	-	-	-	-
Kilkenny,	-	-	-	-	-	-	-	-	-	-	-	-	-	-	-	-	-	-
King's County,	-	-	-	-	-	-	-	-	-	-	-	-	-	-	-	-	-	-
Longford,	-	-	-	-	-	-	-	-	-	-	-	-	-	-	-	-	-	-
Louth,	-	-	-	-	-	-	-	-	-	-	-	-	-	-	-	-	-	-
Meath,	-	-	-	-	-	-	-	-	-	-	-	-	-	-	-	-	-	-
Queen's County,	-	-	-	-	-	-	-	-	-	-	-	-	-	-	-	-	-	-
Westmeath,	-	-	-	-	-	-	-	-	-	-	-	-	-	-	-	-	-	-
Wexford,	[illegible]	-	[illegible]	-	-	[illegible]	-	-	-	-	-	-	-	-	-	-	-	-
Wicklow,	-	-	-	-	-	-	-	-	-	-	-	-	-	-	-	-	-	-
Total of Leinster,	[illegible]	-	[illegible]	-	-	[illegible]	-	-	-	-	-	-	-	-	-	-	-	-

Year 1898 under the Landlord and Tenant (Ireland) Act, 1870, from Returns made of the Peace.

Appeals under Land Sections.															COUNTIES, ARRANGED BY PROVINCES.
Amount Decreed at Sessions.							[illegible] on Appeal.		[illegible] on Appeal.		Amount Decreed at Assizes or by Judges of Consolidated [illegible] Court.				
[illegible]	[illegible]	[illegible]	[illegible]	[illegible]	[illegible]	[illegible]	[illegible]	[illegible]	[illegible]	[illegible]	[illegible]	[illegible]	[illegible]	[illegible]	
															LEINSTER:
-	-	-	-	-	-	-	-	-	-	-	-	-	-	-	Carlow.
-	-	-	-	-	-	-	-	-	-	-	-	-	-	-	Dublin.
-	-	-	-	-	-	-	-	-	-	-	-	-	-	-	Kildare.
-	-	-	-	-	-	-	-	-	-	-	-	-	-	-	Kilkenny.
-	-	-	-	-	-	-	-	-	-	-	-	-	-	-	King's County.
-	-	-	-	-	-	-	-	-	-	-	-	-	-	-	Longford.
-	-	-	-	-	-	-	-	-	-	-	-	-	-	-	Louth.
-	-	-	-	-	-	-	-	-	-	-	-	-	-	-	Meath.
-	-	-	-	-	-	-	-	-	-	-	-	-	-	-	Queen's County.
-	-	-	-	-	-	-	-	-	-	-	-	-	-	-	Westmeath.
-	-	-	-	-	-	-	-	-	-	-	-	-	-	-	Wexford.
-	-	-	-	-	-	-	-	-	-	-	-	-	-	-	Wicklow.
-	-	-	-	-	-	-	-	-	-	-	-	-	-	-	Total of LEINSTER.
															MUNSTER:
-	-	-	-	-	-	-	-	-	-	-	-	-	-	-	Clare.
-	-	-	-	-	-	-	-	-	-	-	-	-	-	-	Cork, E.R.
-	-	-	-	-	-	-	-	-	-	-	-	-	-	-	Cork, W.R.
-	-	-	-	-	-	-	-	-	-	-	-	-	-	-	Kerry.
-	-	-	-	-	-	-	-	-	-	-	-	-	-	-	Limerick.
-	-	-	-	-	-	-	-	-	-	-	-	-	-	-	Tipperary.
-	-	-	-	-	-	-	-	-	-	-	-	-	-	-	Waterford.
-	-	-	-	-	-	-	-	-	-	-	-	-	-	-	Total of MUNSTER.
															ULSTER:
-	-	-	-	-	-	-	-	-	-	-	-	-	-	-	Antrim.
-	-	-	-	-	-	-	-	-	-	-	-	-	-	-	Armagh.
-	-	-	-	-	-	-	-	-	-	-	-	-	-	-	Cavan.
-	-	-	-	-	-	-	-	-	-	-	-	-	-	-	Donegal.
-	-	-	-	-	-	-	-	-	-	-	-	-	-	-	Down.
-	-	-	-	-	-	-	-	-	-	-	-	-	-	-	Fermanagh.
-	-	-	-	-	-	-	-	-	-	-	-	-	-	-	Londonderry.
-	-	-	-	-	-	-	-	-	-	-	-	-	-	-	Monaghan.
-	-	-	-	-	-	-	-	-	-	-	-	-	-	-	Tyrone.
-	-	-	-	-	-	-	-	-	-	-	-	-	-	-	Total of ULSTER.
															CONNAUGHT:
-	-	-	-	-	-	-	-	-	-	-	-	-	-	-	Galway.
-	-	-	-	-	-	-	-	-	-	-	-	-	-	-	Leitrim.
-	-	-	-	-	-	-	-	-	-	-	-	-	-	-	Mayo.
-	-	-	-	-	-	-	-	-	-	-	-	-	-	-	Roscommon.
-	-	-	-	-	-	-	-	-	-	-	-	-	-	-	Sligo.
-	-	-	-	-	-	-	-	-	-	-	-	-	-	-	Total of CONNAUGHT.
-	-	-	-	-	-	-	-	-	-	-	-	-	-	-	Total of IRELAND.

TABLE 44.—Return of Proceedings under

Counties, arranged by Provinces.	Agreements to Fix Fair Rents Filed — First Statutory Term — In Court					Out of Court	Total	Second Statutory Term — In Court				
	[illegible]	[illegible]	[illegible]	[illegible]	[illegible]	[illegible]	[illegible]	[illegible]	[illegible]	[illegible]	[illegible]	[illegible]
LEINSTER:												
Carlow,	[illegible]	[illegible]	[illegible]	.	[illegible]	[illegible]	[illegible]	[illegible]	[illegible]	[illegible]	[illegible]	[illegible]
Dublin,	[illegible]	[illegible]	[illegible]	.	[illegible]	[illegible]	[illegible]	[illegible]	[illegible]	.	.	[illegible]
Kildare,	[illegible]	[illegible]	[illegible]	[illegible]	[illegible]	[illegible]	[illegible]	[illegible]	[illegible]	[illegible]	.	[illegible]
Kilkenny,	[illegible]	[illegible]	[illegible]	.	[illegible]	[illegible]	[illegible]	[illegible]	[illegible]	[illegible]	[illegible]	[illegible]
King's County,	[illegible]	[illegible]	[illegible]	[illegible]	[illegible]	[illegible]	[illegible]	[illegible]	[illegible]	[illegible]	[illegible]	[illegible]
Longford,	[illegible]	[illegible]	[illegible]	[illegible]	[illegible]	[illegible]	[illegible]	[illegible]	[illegible]	[illegible]	[illegible]	[illegible]
Louth,	[illegible]	[illegible]	[illegible]	.	[illegible]	[illegible]	[illegible]	[illegible]	[illegible]	[illegible]		[illegible]
Meath,	[illegible]	[illegible]	[illegible]	.	[illegible]	[illegible]	[illegible]	[illegible]	[illegible]	[illegible]	.	[illegible]
Queen's County,	[illegible]	[illegible]	[illegible]	.	[illegible]	[illegible]	[illegible]	[illegible]	[illegible]	[illegible]	.	[illegible]
Westmeath,	[illegible]	[illegible]	[illegible]	[illegible]	[illegible]	[illegible]	[illegible]	[illegible]	[illegible]	[illegible]	1	[illegible]
Wexford,	[illegible]	[illegible]	[illegible]	[illegible]	[illegible]	[illegible]	[illegible]	[illegible]	[illegible]	[illegible]	[illegible]	[illegible]
Wicklow,	[illegible]	[illegible]	[illegible]	.	[illegible]	[illegible]	[illegible]	[illegible]	[illegible]	[illegible]	[illegible]	[illegible]
Total of Leinster,	[illegible]	[illegible]	[illegible]	[illegible]	[illegible]	[illegible]	[illegible]	[illegible]	[illegible]	[illegible]	[illegible]	[illegible]
MUNSTER:												
Clare,	[illegible]	[illegible]	[illegible]	[illegible]	[illegible]	[illegible]	[illegible]	[illegible]	[illegible]	[illegible]	[illegible]	[illegible]
Cork,	[illegible]	[illegible]	[illegible]	[illegible]	[illegible]	[illegible]	[illegible]	[illegible]	[illegible]	[illegible]	[illegible]	[illegible]
Kerry,	[illegible]	[illegible]	[illegible]	[illegible]	[illegible]	[illegible]	[illegible]	[illegible]	[illegible]	[illegible]	.	[illegible]
Limerick,	[illegible]	[illegible]	[illegible]	[illegible]	[illegible]	[illegible]	[illegible]	[illegible]	[illegible]	[illegible]	[illegible]	[illegible]
Tipperary,	[illegible]	[illegible]	[illegible]	[illegible]	[illegible]	[illegible]	[illegible]	[illegible]	[illegible]	[illegible]	[illegible]	[illegible]
Waterford,	[illegible]	[illegible]	[illegible]	.	[illegible]	[illegible]	[illegible]	[illegible]	[illegible]	[illegible]	[illegible]	[illegible]
Total of Munster,	[illegible]	[illegible]	[illegible]	[illegible]	[illegible]	[illegible]	[illegible]	[illegible]	[illegible]	[illegible]	[illegible]	[illegible]
ULSTER:												
Antrim,	[illegible]	[illegible]	[illegible]	[illegible]	[illegible]	[illegible]	[illegible]	[illegible]	[illegible]	[illegible]	[illegible]	[illegible]
Armagh,	[illegible]	[illegible]	[illegible]	[illegible]	[illegible]	[illegible]	[illegible]	[illegible]	[illegible]	[illegible]	[illegible]	[illegible]
Cavan,	[illegible]	[illegible]	[illegible]	[illegible]	[illegible]	[illegible]	[illegible]	[illegible]	[illegible]	[illegible]	[illegible]	[illegible]
Donegal,	[illegible]	[illegible]	[illegible]	[illegible]	[illegible]	[illegible]	[illegible]	[illegible]	[illegible]	[illegible]	[illegible]	[illegible]
Down,	[illegible]	[illegible]	[illegible]	[illegible]	[illegible]	[illegible]	[illegible]	[illegible]	[illegible]	[illegible]	[illegible]	[illegible]
Fermanagh,	[illegible]	[illegible]	[illegible]	[illegible]	[illegible]	[illegible]	[illegible]	[illegible]	[illegible]	[illegible]	[illegible]	[illegible]
Londonderry,	[illegible]	[illegible]	[illegible]	[illegible]	[illegible]	[illegible]	[illegible]	[illegible]	[illegible]	[illegible]	[illegible]	[illegible]
Monaghan,	[illegible]	[illegible]	[illegible]	[illegible]	[illegible]	[illegible]	[illegible]	[illegible]	[illegible]	[illegible]	.	[illegible]
Tyrone,	[illegible]	[illegible]	[illegible]	[illegible]	[illegible]	[illegible]	[illegible]	[illegible]	[illegible]	[illegible]	[illegible]	[illegible]
Total of Ulster,	[illegible]	[illegible]	[illegible]	[illegible]	[illegible]	[illegible]	[illegible]	[illegible]	[illegible]	[illegible]	[illegible]	[illegible]
CONNAUGHT:												
Galway,	[illegible]	[illegible]	[illegible]	[illegible]	[illegible]	[illegible]	[illegible]	[illegible]	[illegible]	[illegible]	[illegible]	[illegible]
Leitrim,	[illegible]	[illegible]	[illegible]	[illegible]	[illegible]	[illegible]	[illegible]	[illegible]	[illegible]	[illegible]	[illegible]	[illegible]
Mayo,	[illegible]	[illegible]	[illegible]	[illegible]	[illegible]	[illegible]	[illegible]	[illegible]	[illegible]	[illegible]	[illegible]	[illegible]
Roscommon,	[illegible]	[illegible]	[illegible]	[illegible]	[illegible]	[illegible]	[illegible]	[illegible]	[illegible]	[illegible]	.	[illegible]
Sligo,	[illegible]	[illegible]	[illegible]	[illegible]	[illegible]	[illegible]	[illegible]	[illegible]	[illegible]	[illegible]	[illegible]	[illegible]
Total of Connaught,	[illegible]	[illegible]	[illegible]	[illegible]	[illegible]	[illegible]	[illegible]	[illegible]	[illegible]	[illegible]	[illegible]	[illegible]
Total of Ireland,	[illegible]	[illegible]	[illegible]	[illegible]	[illegible]	[illegible]	[illegible]	[illegible]	[illegible]	[illegible]	[illegible]	[illegible]

the Land Law Acts for the Year 1898.

[illegible]	[illegible]	[illegible]	Miscellaneous Proceedings: Number lodged	Disposed of	Number pending at end of year	Appeals on Fair Rent, &c.: First Statutory Term: Number lodged	Heard	Withdrawn	Pending at end of year	Second Statutory Term: Number lodged	Heard	Withdrawn	Pending at end of year	COUNTIES, ARRANGED IN PROVINCES
														LEINSTER:
[illegible]	[illegible]	[illegible]	[illegible]	[illegible]	[illegible]	[illegible]	[illegible]	[illegible]	[illegible]	[illegible]	[illegible]	[illegible]	[illegible]	Carlow.
[illegible]	[illegible]	[illegible]	[illegible]	[illegible]	[illegible]	[illegible]	[illegible]	[illegible]	[illegible]	[illegible]	[illegible]	[illegible]	[illegible]	Dublin.
[illegible]	[illegible]	[illegible]	[illegible]	[illegible]	[illegible]	[illegible]	[illegible]	[illegible]	[illegible]	[illegible]	[illegible]	[illegible]	[illegible]	Kildare.
[illegible]	[illegible]	[illegible]	[illegible]	[illegible]	[illegible]	[illegible]	[illegible]	[illegible]	[illegible]	[illegible]	[illegible]	[illegible]	[illegible]	Kilkenny.
[illegible]	[illegible]	[illegible]	[illegible]	[illegible]	[illegible]	[illegible]	[illegible]	[illegible]	[illegible]	[illegible]	[illegible]	[illegible]	[illegible]	King's County.
[illegible]	[illegible]	[illegible]	[illegible]	[illegible]	[illegible]	[illegible]	[illegible]	[illegible]	[illegible]	[illegible]	[illegible]	[illegible]	[illegible]	Longford.
[illegible]	[illegible]	[illegible]	[illegible]	[illegible]	[illegible]	[illegible]	[illegible]	[illegible]	[illegible]	[illegible]	[illegible]	[illegible]	[illegible]	Louth.
[illegible]	[illegible]	[illegible]	[illegible]	[illegible]	[illegible]	[illegible]	[illegible]	[illegible]	[illegible]	[illegible]	[illegible]	[illegible]	[illegible]	Meath.
[illegible]	[illegible]	[illegible]	[illegible]	[illegible]	[illegible]	[illegible]	[illegible]	[illegible]	[illegible]	[illegible]	[illegible]	[illegible]	[illegible]	Queen's County.
[illegible]	[illegible]	[illegible]	[illegible]	[illegible]	[illegible]	[illegible]	[illegible]	[illegible]	[illegible]	[illegible]	[illegible]	[illegible]	[illegible]	Westmeath.
[illegible]	[illegible]	[illegible]	[illegible]	[illegible]	[illegible]	[illegible]	[illegible]	[illegible]	[illegible]	[illegible]	[illegible]	[illegible]	[illegible]	Wexford.
[illegible]	[illegible]	[illegible]	[illegible]	[illegible]	[illegible]	[illegible]	[illegible]	[illegible]	[illegible]	[illegible]	[illegible]	[illegible]	[illegible]	Wicklow.
[illegible]	[illegible]	[illegible]	[illegible]	[illegible]	[illegible]	[illegible]	[illegible]	[illegible]	[illegible]	[illegible]	[illegible]	[illegible]	[illegible]	Total of Leinster.
														MUNSTER:
[illegible]	[illegible]	[illegible]	[illegible]	[illegible]	[illegible]	[illegible]	[illegible]	[illegible]	[illegible]	[illegible]	[illegible]	[illegible]	[illegible]	Clare.
[illegible]	[illegible]	[illegible]	[illegible]	[illegible]	[illegible]	[illegible]	[illegible]	[illegible]	[illegible]	[illegible]	[illegible]	[illegible]	[illegible]	Cork.
[illegible]	[illegible]	[illegible]	[illegible]	[illegible]	[illegible]	[illegible]	[illegible]	[illegible]	[illegible]	[illegible]	[illegible]	[illegible]	[illegible]	Kerry.
[illegible]	[illegible]	[illegible]	[illegible]	[illegible]	[illegible]	[illegible]	[illegible]	[illegible]	[illegible]	[illegible]	[illegible]	[illegible]	[illegible]	Limerick.
[illegible]	[illegible]	[illegible]	[illegible]	[illegible]	[illegible]	[illegible]	[illegible]	[illegible]	[illegible]	[illegible]	[illegible]	[illegible]	[illegible]	Tipperary.
[illegible]	[illegible]	[illegible]	[illegible]	[illegible]	[illegible]	[illegible]	[illegible]	[illegible]	[illegible]	[illegible]	[illegible]	[illegible]	[illegible]	Waterford.
[illegible]	[illegible]	[illegible]	[illegible]	[illegible]	[illegible]	[illegible]	[illegible]	[illegible]	[illegible]	[illegible]	[illegible]	[illegible]	[illegible]	Total of Munster.
														ULSTER:
[illegible]	[illegible]	[illegible]	[illegible]	[illegible]	[illegible]	[illegible]	[illegible]	[illegible]	[illegible]	[illegible]	[illegible]	[illegible]	[illegible]	Antrim.
[illegible]	[illegible]	[illegible]	[illegible]	[illegible]	[illegible]	[illegible]	[illegible]	[illegible]	[illegible]	[illegible]	[illegible]	[illegible]	[illegible]	Armagh.
[illegible]	[illegible]	[illegible]	[illegible]	[illegible]	[illegible]	[illegible]	[illegible]	[illegible]	[illegible]	[illegible]	[illegible]	[illegible]	[illegible]	Cavan.
[illegible]	[illegible]	[illegible]	[illegible]	[illegible]	[illegible]	[illegible]	[illegible]	[illegible]	[illegible]	[illegible]	[illegible]	[illegible]	[illegible]	Donegal.
[illegible]	[illegible]	[illegible]	[illegible]	[illegible]	[illegible]	[illegible]	[illegible]	[illegible]	[illegible]	[illegible]	[illegible]	[illegible]	[illegible]	Down.
[illegible]	[illegible]	[illegible]	[illegible]	[illegible]	[illegible]	[illegible]	[illegible]	[illegible]	[illegible]	[illegible]	[illegible]	[illegible]	[illegible]	Fermanagh.
[illegible]	[illegible]	[illegible]	[illegible]	[illegible]	[illegible]	[illegible]	[illegible]	[illegible]	[illegible]	[illegible]	[illegible]	[illegible]	[illegible]	Londonderry.
[illegible]	[illegible]	[illegible]	[illegible]	[illegible]	[illegible]	[illegible]	[illegible]	[illegible]	[illegible]	[illegible]	[illegible]	[illegible]	[illegible]	Monaghan.
[illegible]	[illegible]	[illegible]	[illegible]	[illegible]	[illegible]	[illegible]	[illegible]	[illegible]	[illegible]	[illegible]	[illegible]	[illegible]	[illegible]	Tyrone.
[illegible]	[illegible]	[illegible]	[illegible]	[illegible]	[illegible]	[illegible]	[illegible]	[illegible]	[illegible]	[illegible]	[illegible]	[illegible]	[illegible]	Total of Ulster.
														CONNAUGHT:
[illegible]	[illegible]	[illegible]	[illegible]	[illegible]	[illegible]	[illegible]	[illegible]	[illegible]	[illegible]	[illegible]	[illegible]	[illegible]	[illegible]	Galway.
[illegible]	[illegible]	[illegible]	[illegible]	[illegible]	[illegible]	[illegible]	[illegible]	[illegible]	[illegible]	[illegible]	[illegible]	[illegible]	[illegible]	Leitrim.
[illegible]	[illegible]	[illegible]	[illegible]	[illegible]	[illegible]	[illegible]	[illegible]	[illegible]	[illegible]	[illegible]	[illegible]	[illegible]	[illegible]	Mayo.
[illegible]	[illegible]	[illegible]	[illegible]	[illegible]	[illegible]	[illegible]	[illegible]	[illegible]	[illegible]	[illegible]	[illegible]	[illegible]	[illegible]	Roscommon.
[illegible]	[illegible]	[illegible]	[illegible]	[illegible]	[illegible]	[illegible]	[illegible]	[illegible]	[illegible]	[illegible]	[illegible]	[illegible]	[illegible]	Sligo.
[illegible]	[illegible]	[illegible]	[illegible]	[illegible]	[illegible]	[illegible]	[illegible]	[illegible]	[illegible]	[illegible]	[illegible]	[illegible]	[illegible]	Total of Connaught.
[illegible]	[illegible]	[illegible]	[illegible]	[illegible]	[illegible]	[illegible]	[illegible]	[illegible]	[illegible]	[illegible]	[illegible]	[illegible]	[illegible]	Total of Ireland.

TABLE 36—continued.—Return of Proceedings under

Counties, arranged in Provinces.	[illegible]	[illegible]	[illegible]	[illegible]	[illegible]	[illegible]	[illegible]	[illegible]	[illegible]	[illegible]	[illegible]	[illegible]
									£ s. d.	£ s. d.	£ s. d.	£ s. d.
LEINSTER:												
Carlow,	[illegible]	[illegible]	[illegible]	[illegible]	[illegible]	[illegible]	[illegible]	[illegible]	[illegible]	[illegible]	[illegible]	[illegible]
Dublin,	[illegible]	[illegible]	[illegible]	[illegible]	[illegible]	[illegible]	[illegible]	[illegible]	[illegible]	[illegible]	[illegible]	[illegible]
Kildare,	[illegible]	[illegible]	[illegible]	[illegible]	[illegible]	[illegible]	[illegible]	[illegible]	[illegible]	[illegible]	[illegible]	[illegible]
Kilkenny,	[illegible]	[illegible]	[illegible]	[illegible]	[illegible]	[illegible]	[illegible]	[illegible]	[illegible]	[illegible]	[illegible]	[illegible]
King's County,	[illegible]	[illegible]	[illegible]	[illegible]	[illegible]	[illegible]	[illegible]	[illegible]	[illegible]	[illegible]	[illegible]	[illegible]
Longford,	[illegible]	[illegible]	[illegible]	[illegible]	[illegible]	[illegible]	[illegible]	[illegible]	[illegible]	[illegible]	[illegible]	[illegible]
Louth,	[illegible]	[illegible]	[illegible]	[illegible]	[illegible]	[illegible]	[illegible]	[illegible]	[illegible]	[illegible]	[illegible]	[illegible]
Meath,	[illegible]	[illegible]	[illegible]	[illegible]	[illegible]	[illegible]	[illegible]	[illegible]	[illegible]	[illegible]	[illegible]	[illegible]
Queen's County,	[illegible]	[illegible]	[illegible]	[illegible]	[illegible]	[illegible]	[illegible]	[illegible]	[illegible]	[illegible]	[illegible]	[illegible]
Westmeath,	[illegible]	[illegible]	[illegible]	[illegible]	[illegible]	[illegible]	[illegible]	[illegible]	[illegible]	[illegible]	[illegible]	[illegible]
Wexford,	[illegible]	[illegible]	[illegible]	[illegible]	[illegible]	[illegible]	[illegible]	[illegible]	[illegible]	[illegible]	[illegible]	[illegible]
Wicklow,	[illegible]	[illegible]	[illegible]	[illegible]	[illegible]	[illegible]	[illegible]	[illegible]	[illegible]	[illegible]	[illegible]	[illegible]
Total of LEINSTER,	[illegible]	[illegible]	[illegible]	[illegible]	[illegible]	[illegible]	[illegible]	[illegible]	[illegible]	[illegible]	[illegible]	[illegible]
MUNSTER:												
Clare,	[illegible]	[illegible]	[illegible]	[illegible]	[illegible]	[illegible]	[illegible]	[illegible]	[illegible]	[illegible]	[illegible]	[illegible]
Cork,	[illegible]	[illegible]	[illegible]	[illegible]	[illegible]	[illegible]	[illegible]	[illegible]	[illegible]	[illegible]	[illegible]	[illegible]
Kerry,	[illegible]	[illegible]	[illegible]	[illegible]	[illegible]	[illegible]	[illegible]	[illegible]	[illegible]	[illegible]	[illegible]	[illegible]
Limerick,	[illegible]	[illegible]	[illegible]	[illegible]	[illegible]	[illegible]	[illegible]	[illegible]	[illegible]	[illegible]	[illegible]	[illegible]
Tipperary,	[illegible]	[illegible]	[illegible]	[illegible]	[illegible]	[illegible]	[illegible]	[illegible]	[illegible]	[illegible]	[illegible]	[illegible]
Waterford,	[illegible]	[illegible]	[illegible]	[illegible]	[illegible]	[illegible]	[illegible]	[illegible]	[illegible]	[illegible]	[illegible]	[illegible]
Total of MUNSTER,	[illegible]	[illegible]	[illegible]	[illegible]	[illegible]	[illegible]	[illegible]	[illegible]	[illegible]	[illegible]	[illegible]	[illegible]
ULSTER:												
Antrim,	[illegible]	[illegible]	[illegible]	[illegible]	[illegible]	[illegible]	[illegible]	[illegible]	[illegible]	[illegible]	[illegible]	[illegible]
Armagh,	[illegible]	[illegible]	[illegible]	[illegible]	[illegible]	[illegible]	[illegible]	[illegible]	[illegible]	[illegible]	[illegible]	[illegible]
Cavan,	[illegible]	[illegible]	[illegible]	[illegible]	[illegible]	[illegible]	[illegible]	[illegible]	[illegible]	[illegible]	[illegible]	[illegible]
Donegal,	[illegible]	[illegible]	[illegible]	[illegible]	[illegible]	[illegible]	[illegible]	[illegible]	[illegible]	[illegible]	[illegible]	[illegible]
Down,	[illegible]	[illegible]	[illegible]	[illegible]	[illegible]	[illegible]	[illegible]	[illegible]	[illegible]	[illegible]	[illegible]	[illegible]
Fermanagh,	[illegible]	[illegible]	[illegible]	[illegible]	[illegible]	[illegible]	[illegible]	[illegible]	[illegible]	[illegible]	[illegible]	[illegible]
Londonderry,	[illegible]	[illegible]	[illegible]	[illegible]	[illegible]	[illegible]	[illegible]	[illegible]	[illegible]	[illegible]	[illegible]	[illegible]
Monaghan,	[illegible]	[illegible]	[illegible]	[illegible]	[illegible]	[illegible]	[illegible]	[illegible]	[illegible]	[illegible]	[illegible]	[illegible]
Tyrone,	[illegible]	[illegible]	[illegible]	[illegible]	[illegible]	[illegible]	[illegible]	[illegible]	[illegible]	[illegible]	[illegible]	[illegible]
Total of ULSTER,	[illegible]	[illegible]	[illegible]	[illegible]	[illegible]	[illegible]	[illegible]	[illegible]	[illegible]	[illegible]	[illegible]	[illegible]
CONNAUGHT:												
Galway,	[illegible]	[illegible]	[illegible]	[illegible]	[illegible]	[illegible]	[illegible]	[illegible]	[illegible]	[illegible]	[illegible]	[illegible]
Leitrim,	[illegible]	[illegible]	[illegible]	[illegible]	[illegible]	[illegible]	[illegible]	[illegible]	[illegible]	[illegible]	[illegible]	[illegible]
Mayo,	[illegible]	[illegible]	[illegible]	[illegible]	[illegible]	[illegible]	[illegible]	[illegible]	[illegible]	[illegible]	[illegible]	[illegible]
Roscommon,	[illegible]	[illegible]	[illegible]	[illegible]	[illegible]	[illegible]	[illegible]	[illegible]	[illegible]	[illegible]	[illegible]	[illegible]
Sligo,	[illegible]	[illegible]	[illegible]	[illegible]	[illegible]	[illegible]	[illegible]	[illegible]	[illegible]	[illegible]	[illegible]	[illegible]
Total of CONNAUGHT,	[illegible]	[illegible]	[illegible]	[illegible]	[illegible]	[illegible]	[illegible]	[illegible]	[illegible]	[illegible]	[illegible]	[illegible]
Total of IRELAND,	[illegible]	[illegible]	[illegible]	[illegible]	[illegible]	[illegible]	[illegible]	[illegible]	[illegible]	[illegible]	[illegible]	[illegible]

the Land Law Acts for the Year 189[illegible].

Rents.				Terms.				
Second Statutory Term.				First Statutory Term.		Second Statutory Term.		COUNTIES, ARRANGED IN PROVINCES.
In Court.		Out of Court.						
Judicial Rent for First Statutory Term.	Judicial Rent for Second Statutory Term.	Judicial Rent for First Statutory Term.	Judicial Rent for Second Statutory Term.	Former Rent.	Judicial Rent.	Judicial Rent for First Statutory Term.	Judicial Rent for Second Statutory Term.	
£ s. d.	£ s. d.	£ s. d.	£ s. d.	£ s. d.	£ s. d.	£ s. d.	£ s. d.	LEINSTER:
[illegible]	[illegible]	[illegible]	[illegible]	[illegible]	[illegible]	[illegible]	[illegible]	Carlow.
[illegible]	[illegible]	[illegible]	[illegible]	[illegible]	[illegible]	[illegible]	[illegible]	Dublin.
[illegible]	[illegible]	[illegible]	[illegible]	[illegible]	[illegible]	[illegible]	[illegible]	Kildare.
[illegible]	[illegible]	[illegible]	[illegible]	[illegible]	[illegible]	[illegible]	[illegible]	Kilkenny.
[illegible]	[illegible]	[illegible]	[illegible]	[illegible]	[illegible]	[illegible]	[illegible]	King's County.
[illegible]	[illegible]	[illegible]	[illegible]	[illegible]	[illegible]	[illegible]	[illegible]	Longford.
[illegible]	[illegible]	[illegible]	[illegible]	[illegible]	[illegible]	[illegible]	[illegible]	Louth.
[illegible]	[illegible]	[illegible]	[illegible]	[illegible]	[illegible]	[illegible]	[illegible]	Meath.
[illegible]	[illegible]	[illegible]	[illegible]	[illegible]	[illegible]	[illegible]	[illegible]	Queen's County.
[illegible]	[illegible]	[illegible]	[illegible]	[illegible]	[illegible]	[illegible]	[illegible]	Westmeath.
[illegible]	[illegible]	[illegible]	[illegible]	[illegible]	[illegible]	[illegible]	[illegible]	Wexford.
[illegible]	[illegible]	[illegible]	[illegible]	[illegible]	[illegible]	[illegible]	[illegible]	Wicklow.
[illegible]	[illegible]	[illegible]	[illegible]	[illegible]	[illegible]	[illegible]	[illegible]	Total of LEINSTER.
								MUNSTER:
[illegible]	[illegible]	[illegible]	[illegible]	[illegible]	[illegible]	[illegible]	[illegible]	Clare.
[illegible]	[illegible]	[illegible]	[illegible]	[illegible]	[illegible]	[illegible]	[illegible]	Cork.
[illegible]	[illegible]	[illegible]	[illegible]	[illegible]	[illegible]	[illegible]	[illegible]	Kerry.
[illegible]	[illegible]	[illegible]	[illegible]	[illegible]	[illegible]	[illegible]	[illegible]	Limerick.
[illegible]	[illegible]	[illegible]	[illegible]	[illegible]	[illegible]	[illegible]	[illegible]	Tipperary.
[illegible]	[illegible]	[illegible]	[illegible]	[illegible]	[illegible]	[illegible]	[illegible]	Waterford.
[illegible]	[illegible]	[illegible]	[illegible]	[illegible]	[illegible]	[illegible]	[illegible]	Total of MUNSTER.
								ULSTER:
[illegible]	[illegible]	[illegible]	[illegible]	[illegible]	[illegible]	[illegible]	[illegible]	Antrim.
[illegible]	[illegible]	[illegible]	[illegible]	[illegible]	[illegible]	[illegible]	[illegible]	Armagh.
[illegible]	[illegible]	[illegible]	[illegible]	[illegible]	[illegible]	[illegible]	[illegible]	Cavan.
[illegible]	[illegible]	[illegible]	[illegible]	[illegible]	[illegible]	[illegible]	[illegible]	Donegal.
[illegible]	[illegible]	[illegible]	[illegible]	[illegible]	[illegible]	[illegible]	[illegible]	Down.
[illegible]	[illegible]	[illegible]	[illegible]	[illegible]	[illegible]	[illegible]	[illegible]	Fermanagh.
[illegible]	[illegible]	[illegible]	[illegible]	[illegible]	[illegible]	[illegible]	[illegible]	Londonderry.
[illegible]	[illegible]	[illegible]	[illegible]	[illegible]	[illegible]	[illegible]	[illegible]	Monaghan.
[illegible]	[illegible]	[illegible]	[illegible]	[illegible]	[illegible]	[illegible]	[illegible]	Tyrone.
[illegible]	[illegible]	[illegible]	[illegible]	[illegible]	[illegible]	[illegible]	[illegible]	Total of ULSTER.
								CONNAUGHT:
[illegible]	[illegible]	[illegible]	[illegible]	[illegible]	[illegible]	[illegible]	[illegible]	Galway.
[illegible]	[illegible]	[illegible]	[illegible]	[illegible]	[illegible]	[illegible]	[illegible]	Leitrim.
[illegible]	[illegible]	[illegible]	[illegible]	[illegible]	[illegible]	[illegible]	[illegible]	Mayo.
[illegible]	[illegible]	[illegible]	[illegible]	[illegible]	[illegible]	[illegible]	[illegible]	Roscommon.
[illegible]	[illegible]	[illegible]	[illegible]	[illegible]	[illegible]	[illegible]	[illegible]	Sligo.
[illegible]	[illegible]	[illegible]	[illegible]	[illegible]	[illegible]	[illegible]	[illegible]	Total of CONNAUGHT.
[illegible]	[illegible]	[illegible]	[illegible]	[illegible]	[illegible]	[illegible]	[illegible]	Total of IRELAND.

TABLE 56.—Sheriffs' Proceedings in the Year 1898, from Returns

PROCEEDINGS.	Total of Ireland.	LEINSTER. Total in Leinster.	Carlow.	Drogheda Town.	Dublin.	Dublin City.	Kildare.	Kilkenny.	Kilkenny City.	King's County.	Longford.	Louth.	Meath.	Queen's County.
I.—Proceedings other than those for Ejectment or Taking Possession of Land:														
Courts held for Election of Coroners,	2													
Courts held for Election of Members of Parliament,	2	1				1								
Courts held under Writs of Inquiry,	5	3												
Courts held under Lands Clauses, Companies Act, &c.														
Civil Bill Decrees and Dismisses executed by Sheriff,	[illegible]	[illegible]	242	12	274	1,350	[illegible]	182	[illegible]	363	[illegible]	304	[illegible]	[illegible]
" " by Special Bailiffs,	1,[illegible]	[illegible]	57	8	44	44	21	[illegible]	15	[illegible]	21	5	6	[illegible]
Rules (Conditional) taken,	[illegible]	[illegible]	8					[illegible]						
Persons committed as Sheriff's Bailiffs—														
the Defendants,														
the Wards of the Sea,														
the All other Cases,	8	1												
Writs of Habeas Corpus Proceedings in,														
Writs of De Lunatico Inquirendo, Proceedings in,	8	6				4								
All other Writs not being Writs of Execution	16	6				9								
Applications to Court in Proceedings by way of Interpleader,	38	6	1		5	2								
Issues directed thereon,	20	5	1		2	1								
Replevin Bonds taken, or Affidavits of Value lodged,														
Writs of Execution from High Court of Justice—														
Fieri Facias,	3,[illegible]	[illegible]	48		[illegible]	[illegible]	27	4	16	74	61	66	107	44
Capias ad Satisfaciendum,	[illegible]	[illegible]			3	4							1	
II.—For Ejectment or Taking Possession of Land.														
Total number of Ejectments for Non-payment of Rent,	[illegible]	[illegible]	20	9	[illegible]	18	19	30	3	[illegible]	12	31	36	39
Viz.:—Writs of Habere of High Court of Justice executed by Sheriff,	[illegible]	169	8	2	44	48	2			6	3	4	10	3
Writs of Habere of High Court of Justice executed by Special Bailiffs,	6													
Civil Bill Ejectments executed,	3,[illegible]	[illegible]	10	8	18	[illegible]	18	[illegible]	3	30	10	27	26	36
Total number of Ejectments between Landlord and Tenant, other than for Non-payment of Rent,	[illegible]	[illegible]	3		44	94			2		2		16	
Viz.:—Writs of Habere of High Court of Justice executed by Sheriff,	[illegible]	95			38	48								
Writs of Habere of High Court of Justice executed by Special Bailiffs,	5													
Civil Bill Ejectments executed,	[illegible]	[illegible]	3		18	42			2		12		19	
Total number of Ejectments other than between Landlord and Tenant,	[illegible]	34	4			1					1	9		
Viz.:—Writs of Habere of High Court of Justice executed by Sheriff,	38	3												
Writs of Habere of High Court of Justice executed by Special Bailiffs,	8													
Civil Bill Ejectments executed,	16	14	4			1					6	3		
Total number of Ejectments of all Classes,	[illegible]	[illegible]	33	9	72	160	27	32	6	48	18	40	48	38
Writs of Habere and [illegible] executed by [illegible], [illegible]	9	4				3								
Numbers of [illegible]	38	2				3								
Numbers of Writs of [illegible]														
[illegible]														
Writs of [illegible] from the Chancery Division,	5													
Writs of Assistance from the Probate and Matrimonial Division,														
Injunctions from Land Judges,	6	3								2				
Warrants under Land Clauses Acts,	4	3												
Other Process or Orders,	6	4									2			

by Sheriffs of Counties and of Counties of Cities and of Towns.

* No return.

I.—Proceedings other than those for Recovery of Possession of Land.								
Writs held for Election of Coroners,	[illegible]							
Writs held for Election of Members of Parliament,	[illegible]							[illegible]
Inquests held under Writs of Trial or Inquiry,	[illegible]	[illegible]						
Inquisitions under Land Clauses, Consolidation Act, &c.,	..		..					
Writs of Fieri Facias and Elegits executed by Sheriff,	[illegible]	[illegible]	[illegible]	[illegible]	[illegible]	[illegible]	[illegible]	[illegible]
" " " by Special Bailiffs,	[illegible]	[illegible]	[illegible]	[illegible]		[illegible]	[illegible]	[illegible]
Writs of Capias ad Satisfaciendum,								
Writs of Attachment of Queen's Bench:—								
(1) [illegible]								
(2) [illegible]								
(3) All other Courts,								
Writs of Habeas Corpus, Proceedings &c.,								
Writs of De Lunatico Inquirendo, Proceedings &c.,								
All other Writs, not being Writs of Execution,	[illegible]	[illegible]						
Applications to Sheriffs in Proceedings by way of Interpleader,	[illegible]					[illegible]		
[illegible]								
Replevin Bonds taken, or Affidavits of Value sworn,								
Writs of Execution from High Court of Justice:—								
[illegible]	[illegible]		[illegible]	[illegible]	[illegible]	[illegible]	[illegible]	[illegible]
[illegible]	[illegible]	[illegible]	[illegible]		[illegible]	..		
II.—For Recovery of Landed Possession of Land.								
Total number of Ejectments for Non-payment of Rent,	[illegible]	[illegible]	[illegible]		[illegible]	[illegible]	[illegible]	[illegible]
[illegible]—Writs of Habere of High Court of Justice executed by Sheriff,	[illegible]		[illegible]		[illegible]		[illegible]	[illegible]
" " " by Special Bailiffs,	[illegible]			..				[illegible]
Civil Bill Ejectments executed,	[illegible]	[illegible]	[illegible]		[illegible]	[illegible]	[illegible]	[illegible]
Total Number of Ejectments between Landlord and Tenant, other than for Non-payment of Rent,	[illegible]	[illegible]	[illegible]	[illegible]	[illegible]	[illegible]	[illegible]	[illegible]
[illegible]—Writs of Habere of High Court of Justice executed by Sheriff,	[illegible]		[illegible]	[illegible]				[illegible]
" " " by Special Bailiffs,	[illegible]		..			[illegible]		
Civil Bill Ejectments executed,	[illegible]	[illegible]	[illegible]		[illegible]	[illegible]	[illegible]	[illegible]
Total number of Ejectments other than between Landlord and Tenant,	[illegible]	[illegible]		..	[illegible]	[illegible]		[illegible]
[illegible]—Writs of Habere of High Court of Justice executed by Sheriff,	[illegible]	[illegible]			[illegible]			[illegible]
" " " by Special Bailiffs,	[illegible]					[illegible]		
Civil Bill Ejectments executed,	[illegible]	[illegible]			[illegible]	[illegible]		[illegible]
Total number of Ejectments of all Classes,	[illegible]	[illegible]	[illegible]	[illegible]	[illegible]	[illegible]	[illegible]	[illegible]
[illegible]								
[illegible]								
[illegible]								
[illegible]								
[illegible]								
[illegible]								
[illegible]								
[illegible]								
[illegible]								

Returns by Sheriffs of Counties and of Counties of Cities and of Towns.

Londonderry.	Monaghan.	Tyrone.	Belfast, County of.	Cork.	Drogheda, Town of.	Galway.	Kilkenny.	Limerick.	Waterford.	PROCEEDINGS.
										I.—PROCEEDINGS OTHER THAN THOSE FOR RECOVERY OF POSSESSION OF LAND.
1	.	.	.	.	.	.	.	.	.	Courts held for Election of Coroners.
.	.	.	.	.	.	.	.	.	.	Courts held for Election of Members of Parliament.
.	...	.	.	.	.	.	.	.	.	Courts held under Writs of Trial or Inquiry.
.	.	.	.	.	.	.	.	.	.	Courts held under Land Clauses, Compensation Acts, &c.
908	226	1,481	2727	901	86	171	[illegible]	491	160	Civil Bill Decrees and Warrants executed by Sheriff.
1,597	461	452	695	347	3	31	.	244	64	" " " by Special Bailiffs.
.	..	.	.	.	.	.	.	.	.	Jury Commissions issued.
										Persons reported as [illegible] in—
.	.	.	.	.	.	.	.	.	.	(1) [illegible]
.	.	.	.	.	.	.	.	.	.	(2) Writs of [illegible]
.	.	.	.	.	.	.	.	.	.	(3) All other Cases.
.	.	.	.	.	.	.	.	.	.	Writs of Habeas Corpus, Attachments, &c.
.	.	.	.	.	.	.	.	.	.	Writs in the Exchequer Department, Proceedings in.
.	.	...	2	.	.	1	4	2	.	All other Writs, excluding Writs of Execution.
.	.	.	2	.	.	.	.	1	.	Applications to Court in Proceedings by way of Interpleader.
.	.	..	2	.	.	.	.	1	.	[illegible]
.	.	.	.	.	.	.	.	.	.	Replevin Bonds taken, or Affidavits of Value drawn.
										Writs of Execution from High Court of Justice:—
186	16	.	687	189	37	58	142	297	..	Fieri Facias.
.	8	.	.	.	.	.	.	.	.	Capias ad Satisfaciendum.
										II.—PROCEEDINGS FOR RECOVERY OF POSSESSION OF LAND.
34	38	46	352	85	4	37	59	34	16	Total number of Ejectments for Non-payment of Rent.
.	9	.	74	4	.	.	6	8	1	Viz.:—Writs of Habere of High Court of Justice executed by Sheriff.
.	..	.	.	.	.	.	.	.	.	" " " Special Bailiffs.
11	30	69	238	94	4	37	32	28	13	Civil Bill Ejectments executed.
122	.	34	791	64	3	16	49	37	..	Total number of Ejectments between Landlord and Tenant, other than for Non-payment of Rent.
.	.	7	2	.	.	.	.	3	.	Viz.:—Writs of Habere of High Court of Justice executed by Sheriff.
.	.	.	.	.	.	.	.	.	.	" " " by Special Bailiffs.
126	.	68	190	63	3	16	39	34	20	Civil Bill Ejectments executed.
3	.	.	88	.	.	..	6	12	18	Total number of Ejectments other than between Landlord and Tenant.
5	.	.	5	.	.	.	6	3	1	Viz.:—Writs of Habere of High Court of Justice executed by Sheriff.
.	.	.	.	.	.	.	.	.	.	" " " by Special Bailiffs.
.	.	.	29	.	.	.	.	17	14	Civil Bill Ejectments executed.
146	38	122	942	187	8	49	100	99	50	Total number of Ejectments of all Classes.
.	.	.	3	.	1	.	.	.	.	Writs of Habere and Possession [illegible]
.	.	.	.	.	.	.	.	.	.	Number of [illegible]
.	.	.	.	.	.	.	.	.	.	Number of Writs of [illegible] Partial Exemption [illegible]
.	.	.	.	.	.	.	.	.	.	[illegible]
.	.	.	.	.	.	.	.	.	.	Writs of Assistance from the Chancery Division.
.	.	.	.	.	.	.	.	.	.	Writs of Assistance from the Probate and Matrimonial Division.
.	.	.	.	.	.	.	.	.	.	Injunctions from Land Judges.
.	.	.	.	.	.	.	.	.	.	[illegible]
.	.	.	.	.	.	.	.	.	.	Other Process or Orders.

* No Return.

TABLE 57.—JURORS.—Proceedings of Judges, County Court Judges, and Revising Jurors' List and Jurors' Books, from Returns

Counties, Counties of Cities and Towns, and Boroughs having separate Sessions of the Peace, arranged in Provinces	General Jurors' Lists [illegible]					General Jurors' Books [illegible]	Qualified as				
	Returned in Lists by Clerks of Unions, and in the City of Dublin by the Collector-General	Added by Revising Court	Struck off by Revising Court	[illegible] by Clerk of Peace	Struck off Book by Judges	Total in Book [illegible]	[illegible]	[illegible]	Rated Occupiers	[illegible] of Company	Railway Companies
Leinster:											
Carlow	[illegible]	.	[illegible]	.	.	[illegible]	[illegible]	[illegible]	[illegible]	.	.
Drogheda, Town of	[illegible]	.	[illegible]	.	[illegible]	[illegible]	[illegible]	.	[illegible]	[illegible]	[illegible]
Dublin	[illegible]	[illegible]	[illegible]	[illegible]	.	[illegible]	[illegible]	[illegible]	[illegible]	[illegible]	.
„ City	[illegible]	[illegible]	[illegible]	.	.	[illegible]	[illegible]	[illegible]	[illegible]	[illegible]	.
Kildare	[illegible]	.	[illegible]	.	.	[illegible]	[illegible]	[illegible]	[illegible]	[illegible]	.
Kilkenny	[illegible]	.	[illegible]	.	.	[illegible]	[illegible]	[illegible]	[illegible]	.	.
„ City	[illegible]	.	[illegible]	.	.	[illegible]	.	.	[illegible]	.	.
Kings County	[illegible]	.	[illegible]	.	.	[illegible]	[illegible]	[illegible]	[illegible]	[illegible]	.
Longford	[illegible]	.	[illegible]	.	.	[illegible]	[illegible]	[illegible]	[illegible]	.	.
Louth	[illegible]	.	[illegible]	.	.	[illegible]	[illegible]	.	[illegible]	[illegible]	.
Meath	[illegible]	.	[illegible]	[illegible]	[illegible]	[illegible]	[illegible]	[illegible]	[illegible]	[illegible]	.
Queen's County	[illegible]	.	[illegible]	.	.	[illegible]	[illegible]	[illegible]	[illegible]	[illegible]	.
Westmeath	[illegible]	.	[illegible]	.	.	[illegible]	[illegible]	[illegible]	[illegible]	[illegible]	.
Wexford	[illegible]	.	[illegible]	.	.	[illegible]	[illegible]	[illegible]	[illegible]	[illegible]	[illegible]
Wicklow	[illegible]	.	[illegible]	[illegible]	.	[illegible]	[illegible]	[illegible]	[illegible]	.	.
Total of Leinster	[illegible]	[illegible]	[illegible]	[illegible]	[illegible]	[illegible]	[illegible]	[illegible]	[illegible]	[illegible]	[illegible]
Munster:											
Clare	[illegible]	.	[illegible]	.	.	[illegible]	[illegible]	[illegible]	[illegible]	.	.
Cork, E.R.	[illegible]	.	[illegible]	.	.	[illegible]	[illegible]	[illegible]	[illegible]	[illegible]	[illegible]
„ W.R.	[illegible]	.	[illegible]	.	.	[illegible]	[illegible]	[illegible]	[illegible]	[illegible]	[illegible]
„ City	[illegible]	.	[illegible]	.	.	[illegible]	[illegible]	[illegible]	[illegible]	[illegible]	[illegible]
Kerry	[illegible]	.	[illegible]	.	.	[illegible]	[illegible]	[illegible]	[illegible]	[illegible]	[illegible]
Limerick	[illegible]	.	[illegible]	.	.	[illegible]	[illegible]	[illegible]	[illegible]	.	.
„ City	[illegible]	.	[illegible]	.	.	[illegible]	.	[illegible]	[illegible]	.	.
Tipperary	[illegible]	.	[illegible]	.	.	[illegible]	[illegible]	[illegible]	[illegible]	[illegible]	.
Waterford	[illegible]	.	[illegible]	.	.	[illegible]	[illegible]	[illegible]	[illegible]	[illegible]	[illegible]
„ City	[illegible]	.	[illegible]	.	[illegible]	[illegible]	.	.	[illegible]	[illegible]	.
Total of Munster	[illegible]	.	[illegible]	.	[illegible]	[illegible]	[illegible]	[illegible]	[illegible]	[illegible]	[illegible]
Ulster:											
Antrim	[illegible]	.	[illegible]	.	.	[illegible]	[illegible]	[illegible]	[illegible]	[illegible]	.
Armagh	[illegible]	.	[illegible]	.	[illegible]	[illegible]	[illegible]	[illegible]	[illegible]	[illegible]	.
Belfast, Borough	[illegible]	.	[illegible]	.	.	[illegible]	.	.	[illegible]	.	.
Carrickfergus, Town of	[illegible]	.	[illegible]	.	.	[illegible]	.	.	[illegible]	.	.
Cavan	[illegible]	.	[illegible]	.	.	[illegible]	[illegible]	[illegible]	[illegible]	[illegible]	.
Donegal	[illegible]	.	[illegible]	.	.	[illegible]	[illegible]	[illegible]	[illegible]	[illegible]	.
Down	[illegible]	.	[illegible]	.	.	[illegible]	[illegible]	[illegible]	[illegible]	[illegible]	.
Fermanagh	[illegible]	.	[illegible]	.	.	[illegible]	[illegible]	[illegible]	[illegible]	.	.
Londonderry	[illegible]	.	[illegible]	.	.	[illegible]	[illegible]	[illegible]	[illegible]	.	.
„ Borough	[illegible]	.	[illegible]	.	.	[illegible]	[illegible]	[illegible]	[illegible]	.	.
Monaghan	[illegible]	.	[illegible]	.	.	[illegible]	[illegible]	.	[illegible]	[illegible]	.
Tyrone	[illegible]	.	[illegible]	.	.	[illegible]	[illegible]	[illegible]	[illegible]	.	.
Total of Ulster	[illegible]	.	[illegible]	.	[illegible]	[illegible]	[illegible]	[illegible]	[illegible]	[illegible]	.
Connaught:											
Galway	[illegible]	.	[illegible]	.	.	[illegible]	[illegible]	[illegible]	[illegible]	.	.
„ Town of	[illegible]	.	[illegible]	.	.	[illegible]	.	[illegible]	[illegible]	.	.
Leitrim	[illegible]	.	[illegible]	.	.	[illegible]	[illegible]	[illegible]	[illegible]	[illegible]	.
Mayo	[illegible]	.	[illegible]	.	.	[illegible]	[illegible]	[illegible]	[illegible]	.	.
Roscommon	[illegible]	.	[illegible]	.	.	[illegible]	[illegible]	[illegible]	[illegible]	[illegible]	.
Sligo	[illegible]	.	[illegible]	.	.	[illegible]	[illegible]	[illegible]	[illegible]	.	.
Total of Connaught	[illegible]	.	[illegible]	.	.	[illegible]	[illegible]	[illegible]	[illegible]	[illegible]	.
Total of Ireland	[illegible]	[illegible]	[illegible]	[illegible]	[illegible]	[illegible]	[illegible]	[illegible]	[illegible]	[illegible]	[illegible]

Barristers, in respect of the Preparation, Revision, and Correction, in 1896, of made by the Clerks of the Peace.

Special Jurors' Lists as prepared in 1896: On List as prepared by Clerk of Peace	Added by Revising Court	Struck off by Revising Court	Erroneously by Clerk of Peace	Struck off by Judges	Special Jurors' Book 1896-7: Total on Book when handed to Sheriff	Corrections of Jurors or Special Jurors' Book for 1896: Common Jurors added	Common Jurors expunged or struck off	Special Jurors added	Special Jurors expunged or struck off	Counties, Counties of Cities and Towns, and Boroughs having separate Clerks of the Peace, arranged in Provinces
										LEINSTER:
[illegible]	.	[illegible]	.	.	[illegible]	.	.	.	.	Carlow.
[illegible]	.	[illegible]	.	.	[illegible]	.	4	.	.	Drogheda, Town of.
[illegible]	[illegible]	[illegible]	[illegible]	.	[illegible]	.	.	.	.	Dublin.
[illegible]	[illegible]	[illegible]	.	.	[illegible]	.	.	.	.	Dublin City.
[illegible]	.	[illegible]	.	.	[illegible]	.	.	.	.	Kildare.
[illegible]	.	4	.	.	[illegible]	.	.	.	.	Kilkenny.
[illegible]	.	[illegible]	.	.	[illegible]	.	.	.	.	Kilkenny City.
[illegible]	.	[illegible]	.	.	[illegible]	.	[illegible]	.	[illegible]	King's County.
[illegible]	.	.	.	.	[illegible]	.	.	.	.	Longford.
[illegible]	.	[illegible]	.	.	[illegible]	[illegible]	.	[illegible]	.	Louth.
[illegible]	.	[illegible]	[illegible]	.	[illegible]	.	.	.	.	Meath.
[illegible]	.	[illegible]	.	.	[illegible]	.	[illegible]	.	[illegible]	Queen's County.
[illegible]	[illegible]	.	.	.	[illegible]	.	[illegible]	.	1	Westmeath.
[illegible]	[illegible]	[illegible]	.	.	[illegible]	[illegible]	.	.	[illegible]	Wexford.
[illegible]	.	[illegible]	[illegible]	.	[illegible]	.	.	.	.	Wicklow.
[illegible]	[illegible]	[illegible]	[illegible]	.	[illegible]	[illegible]	[illegible]	[illegible]	[illegible]	Total of Leinster.
										MUNSTER:
[illegible]	.	4	.	.	[illegible]	[illegible]	[illegible]	[illegible]	[illegible]	Clare.
[illegible]	.	[illegible]	.	.	[illegible]	.	[illegible]	.	[illegible]	Cork, E.R.
[illegible]	.	[illegible]	.	.	[illegible]	.	.	.	.	" W.R.
[illegible]	.	[illegible]	.	.	[illegible]	[illegible]	.	.	.	" City.
[illegible]	.	[illegible]	.	.	[illegible]	.	.	.	.	Kerry.
[illegible]	[illegible]	[illegible]	.	.	[illegible]	.	.	.	.	Limerick.
[illegible]	[illegible]	[illegible]	.	.	[illegible]	.	[illegible]	.	[illegible]	" City.
[illegible]	.	[illegible]	.	.	[illegible]	.	.	.	.	Tipperary.
[illegible]	.	[illegible]	.	.	[illegible]	.	.	.	.	Waterford.
[illegible]	.	[illegible]	.	.	[illegible]	.	.	.	.	" City.
[illegible]	[illegible]	[illegible]	.	.	[illegible]	[illegible]	[illegible]	[illegible]	[illegible]	Total of Munster.
										ULSTER:
[illegible]	[illegible]	[illegible]	.	.	[illegible]	.	.	.	.	Antrim.
[illegible]	.	[illegible]	.	[illegible]	[illegible]	.	[illegible]	.	[illegible]	Armagh.
.	.	.	.	.	.	.	.	.	.	Belfast, Borough.
[illegible]	.	[illegible]	.	.	[illegible]	.	.	.	.	Carrickfergus, Town of.
[illegible]	.	[illegible]	.	.	[illegible]	.	[illegible]	.	.	Cavan.
[illegible]	.	[illegible]	.	.	[illegible]	.	[illegible]	.	[illegible]	Donegal.
[illegible]	[illegible]	.	.	.	[illegible]	.	.	.	.	Down.
[illegible]	.	[illegible]	.	.	[illegible]	[illegible]	.	[illegible]	[illegible]	Fermanagh.
[illegible]	.	[illegible]	.	.	[illegible]	.	.	.	.	Londonderry.
[illegible]	.	[illegible]	.	.	[illegible]	.	.	.	.	" Borough.
[illegible]	.	[illegible]	.	.	[illegible]	.	.	.	.	Monaghan.
[illegible]	.	[illegible]	.	.	[illegible]	.	.	.	.	Tyrone.
[illegible]	[illegible]	[illegible]	.	[illegible]	[illegible]	[illegible]	[illegible]	[illegible]	[illegible]	Total of Ulster.
										CONNAUGHT:
[illegible]	.	[illegible]	.	.	[illegible]	.	.	.	.	Galway.
[illegible]	.	[illegible]	.	.	[illegible]	.	[illegible]	.	[illegible]	" Town of.
[illegible]	[illegible]	[illegible]	.	.	[illegible]	.	.	.	.	Leitrim.
[illegible]	.	[illegible]	.	.	[illegible]	.	.	.	.	Mayo.
[illegible]	.	.	.	.	[illegible]	.	.	.	.	Roscommon.
[illegible]	.	[illegible]	.	.	[illegible]	.	.	.	.	Sligo.
[illegible]	[illegible]	[illegible]	.	.	[illegible]	.	[illegible]	.	3	Total of Connaught.
[illegible]	[illegible]	[illegible]	[illegible]	[illegible]	[illegible]	[illegible]	[illegible]	[illegible]	[illegible]	Total of Ireland.

IRELAND.

LE 58.—JURORS.—Proceedings of Sheriffs in summoning Jurors in the Year
Londonderry Boroughs, [illegible]

COUNTIES, COUNTIES OF CITIES AND TOWNS, AND BOROUGHS HAVING SEPARATE SESSIONS OF THE PEACE, ARRANGED IN PROVINCES.	Total Number of Persons summoned during the year	[illegible]								
		Grand Jurors.			Petit and Common Jurors.			Special Jurors.		
		January to June.	July to December.	Total.	January to June.	July to December.	Total.	January to June.	July to December.	Total
[illegible]										
[illegible]										
[illegible]		[illegible]	[illegible]	[illegible]	[illegible]	[illegible]	[illegible]	[illegible]	[illegible]	[illegible]
[illegible]	[illegible]	[illegible]	[illegible]	[illegible]	[illegible]	[illegible]	[illegible]	[illegible]	[illegible]	[illegible]
[illegible]	[illegible]	[illegible]	[illegible]	[illegible]	[illegible]	[illegible]	[illegible]	[illegible]	[illegible]	[illegible]

their Office, 1898-99, from Returns by the Sheriffs, and, in the case of Belfast and the Clerks of the Peace.

For Criminal Offences: Grand Juries: January to June	Grand Juries: July to December	Grand Juries: Total	Petty Juries: January to June	Petty Juries: July to December	Petty Juries: Total	Civil Bill Courts (County Court Judges or Recorders): January to June	July to December	Total	Other Purposes	Counties, Counties of Cities and Towns, and Boroughs having separate Sessions of the Peace, arranged in Provinces
										Leinster: Dublin:
[illegible]	[illegible]	[illegible]	[illegible]	[illegible]	[illegible]	[illegible]		[illegible]	[illegible]	Total of Dublin County
[illegible]	[illegible]	[illegible]	[illegible]	[illegible]	[illegible]				[illegible]	Total of Dublin City
[illegible]	[illegible]	[illegible]	[illegible]	[illegible]	[illegible]	[illegible]	[illegible]	[illegible]	[illegible]	Total of Leinster
										Munster:
[illegible]	[illegible]	[illegible]	[illegible]	[illegible]	[illegible]	[illegible]	[illegible]	[illegible]		Total of Munster
										Ulster:
[illegible]	[illegible]	[illegible]	[illegible]	[illegible]	[illegible]	[illegible]	[illegible]	[illegible]	[illegible]	Total of Ulster
										Connaught:
[illegible]	[illegible]	[illegible]	[illegible]	[illegible]	[illegible]	[illegible]	[illegible]	[illegible]		Total of Connaught
[illegible]	[illegible]	[illegible]	[illegible]	[illegible]	[illegible]	[illegible]	[illegible]	[illegible]	[illegible]	Total of Ireland

[illegible] of Dublin County and Dublin City.

[illegible]	[illegible]	[illegible]
[illegible]	[illegible]	[illegible]
[illegible]	[illegible]	[illegible]

Magistrates and the Number of Civil Cases other than Proceedings as to Cottier to overholding Tenants in Towns under 14 & 15 Vic., c. 92, from Returns made by

[illegible]								[illegible]				[illegible]
[illegible]		[illegible]		[illegible]		[illegible]	[illegible]	[illegible]	[illegible]	[illegible]	[illegible]	
[illegible]	[illegible]	[illegible]	[illegible]	[illegible]	[illegible]							
												LEINSTER.
[illegible]	[illegible]	[illegible]	[illegible]	[illegible]	[illegible]	[illegible]	[illegible]	[illegible]	[illegible]	[illegible]	[illegible]	Carlow.
[illegible]	[illegible]	[illegible]	[illegible]	[illegible]	[illegible]	[illegible]	[illegible]	[illegible]	[illegible]	[illegible]	[illegible]	Drogheda, Town of.
[illegible]	[illegible]	[illegible]	[illegible]	[illegible]	[illegible]	[illegible]	[illegible]	[illegible]	[illegible]	[illegible]	[illegible]	Dublin (outside Metropolitan Police District.)
[illegible]	[illegible]	[illegible]	[illegible]	[illegible]	[illegible]	[illegible]	[illegible]	[illegible]	[illegible]	[illegible]	[illegible]	Dublin (inside Metropolitan Police District.)
[illegible]	[illegible]	[illegible]	[illegible]	[illegible]	[illegible]	[illegible]	[illegible]	[illegible]	[illegible]	[illegible]	[illegible]	Kildare.
[illegible]	[illegible]	[illegible]	[illegible]	[illegible]	[illegible]	[illegible]	[illegible]	[illegible]	[illegible]	[illegible]	[illegible]	Kilkenny.
[illegible]	[illegible]	[illegible]	[illegible]	[illegible]	[illegible]	[illegible]	[illegible]	[illegible]	[illegible]	[illegible]	[illegible]	Kilkenny City.
[illegible]	[illegible]	[illegible]	[illegible]	[illegible]	[illegible]	[illegible]	[illegible]	[illegible]	[illegible]	[illegible]	[illegible]	King's County.
[illegible]	[illegible]	[illegible]	[illegible]	[illegible]	[illegible]	[illegible]	[illegible]	[illegible]	[illegible]	[illegible]	[illegible]	Longford.
[illegible]	[illegible]	[illegible]	[illegible]	[illegible]	[illegible]	[illegible]	[illegible]	[illegible]	[illegible]	[illegible]	[illegible]	Louth.
[illegible]	[illegible]	[illegible]	[illegible]	[illegible]	[illegible]	[illegible]	[illegible]	[illegible]	[illegible]	[illegible]	[illegible]	Meath.
[illegible]	[illegible]	[illegible]	[illegible]	[illegible]	[illegible]	[illegible]	[illegible]	[illegible]	[illegible]	[illegible]	[illegible]	Queen's County.
[illegible]	[illegible]	[illegible]	[illegible]	[illegible]	[illegible]	[illegible]	[illegible]	[illegible]	[illegible]	[illegible]	[illegible]	Westmeath.
[illegible]	[illegible]	[illegible]	[illegible]	[illegible]	[illegible]	[illegible]	[illegible]	[illegible]	[illegible]	[illegible]	[illegible]	Wexford.
[illegible]	[illegible]	[illegible]	[illegible]	[illegible]	[illegible]	[illegible]	[illegible]	[illegible]	[illegible]	[illegible]	[illegible]	Wicklow.
[illegible]	[illegible]	[illegible]	[illegible]	[illegible]	[illegible]	[illegible]	[illegible]	[illegible]	[illegible]	[illegible]	[illegible]	Total.
												MUNSTER.
[illegible]	[illegible]	[illegible]	[illegible]	[illegible]	[illegible]	[illegible]	[illegible]	[illegible]	[illegible]	[illegible]	[illegible]	Clare.
[illegible]	[illegible]	[illegible]	[illegible]	[illegible]	[illegible]	[illegible]	[illegible]	[illegible]	[illegible]	[illegible]	[illegible]	Cork.
[illegible]	[illegible]	[illegible]	[illegible]	[illegible]	[illegible]	[illegible]	[illegible]	[illegible]	[illegible]	[illegible]	[illegible]	Cork City.
[illegible]	[illegible]	[illegible]	[illegible]	[illegible]	[illegible]	[illegible]	[illegible]	[illegible]	[illegible]	[illegible]	[illegible]	Kerry.
[illegible]	[illegible]	[illegible]	[illegible]	[illegible]	[illegible]	[illegible]	[illegible]	[illegible]	[illegible]	[illegible]	[illegible]	Limerick.
[illegible]	[illegible]	[illegible]	[illegible]	[illegible]	[illegible]	[illegible]	[illegible]	[illegible]	[illegible]	[illegible]	[illegible]	Limerick City.
[illegible]	[illegible]	[illegible]	[illegible]	[illegible]	[illegible]	[illegible]	[illegible]	[illegible]	[illegible]	[illegible]	[illegible]	Tipperary.
[illegible]	[illegible]	[illegible]	[illegible]	[illegible]	[illegible]	[illegible]	[illegible]	[illegible]	[illegible]	[illegible]	[illegible]	Waterford.
[illegible]	[illegible]	[illegible]	[illegible]	[illegible]	[illegible]	[illegible]	[illegible]	[illegible]	[illegible]	[illegible]	[illegible]	Waterford City and [illegible].
[illegible]	[illegible]	[illegible]	[illegible]	[illegible]	[illegible]	[illegible]	[illegible]	[illegible]	[illegible]	[illegible]	[illegible]	Total.
												ULSTER.
[illegible]	[illegible]	[illegible]	[illegible]	[illegible]	[illegible]	[illegible]	[illegible]	[illegible]	[illegible]	[illegible]	[illegible]	Antrim.
[illegible]	[illegible]	[illegible]	[illegible]	[illegible]	[illegible]	[illegible]	[illegible]	[illegible]	[illegible]	[illegible]	[illegible]	Armagh.
[illegible]	[illegible]	[illegible]	[illegible]	[illegible]	[illegible]	[illegible]	[illegible]	[illegible]	[illegible]	[illegible]	[illegible]	Carrickfergus, Co. of Town.
[illegible]	[illegible]	[illegible]	[illegible]	[illegible]	[illegible]	[illegible]	[illegible]	[illegible]	[illegible]	[illegible]	[illegible]	Cavan.
[illegible]	[illegible]	[illegible]	[illegible]	[illegible]	[illegible]	[illegible]	[illegible]	[illegible]	[illegible]	[illegible]	[illegible]	Donegal.
[illegible]	[illegible]	[illegible]	[illegible]	[illegible]	[illegible]	[illegible]	[illegible]	[illegible]	[illegible]	[illegible]	[illegible]	Down.
[illegible]	[illegible]	[illegible]	[illegible]	[illegible]	[illegible]	[illegible]	[illegible]	[illegible]	[illegible]	[illegible]	[illegible]	Fermanagh.
[illegible]	[illegible]	[illegible]	[illegible]	[illegible]	[illegible]	[illegible]	[illegible]	[illegible]	[illegible]	[illegible]	[illegible]	Londonderry.
[illegible]	[illegible]	[illegible]	[illegible]	[illegible]	[illegible]	[illegible]	[illegible]	[illegible]	[illegible]	[illegible]	[illegible]	Londonderry City.
[illegible]	[illegible]	[illegible]	[illegible]	[illegible]	[illegible]	[illegible]	[illegible]	[illegible]	[illegible]	[illegible]	[illegible]	Monaghan.
[illegible]	[illegible]	[illegible]	[illegible]	[illegible]	[illegible]	[illegible]	[illegible]	[illegible]	[illegible]	[illegible]	[illegible]	Tyrone.
[illegible]	[illegible]	[illegible]	[illegible]	[illegible]	[illegible]	[illegible]	[illegible]	[illegible]	[illegible]	[illegible]	[illegible]	Total.
												CONNAUGHT.
[illegible]	[illegible]	[illegible]	[illegible]	[illegible]	[illegible]	[illegible]	[illegible]	[illegible]	[illegible]	[illegible]	[illegible]	Galway.
[illegible]	[illegible]	[illegible]	[illegible]	[illegible]	[illegible]	[illegible]	[illegible]	[illegible]	[illegible]	[illegible]	[illegible]	Galway (Co. of Town.)
[illegible]	[illegible]	[illegible]	[illegible]	[illegible]	[illegible]	[illegible]	[illegible]	[illegible]	[illegible]	[illegible]	[illegible]	Leitrim.
[illegible]	[illegible]	[illegible]	[illegible]	[illegible]	[illegible]	[illegible]	[illegible]	[illegible]	[illegible]	[illegible]	[illegible]	Mayo.
[illegible]	[illegible]	[illegible]	[illegible]	[illegible]	[illegible]	[illegible]	[illegible]	[illegible]	[illegible]	[illegible]	[illegible]	Roscommon.
[illegible]	[illegible]	[illegible]	[illegible]	[illegible]	[illegible]	[illegible]	[illegible]	[illegible]	[illegible]	[illegible]	[illegible]	Sligo.
[illegible]	[illegible]	[illegible]	[illegible]	[illegible]	[illegible]	[illegible]	[illegible]	[illegible]	[illegible]	[illegible]	[illegible]	Total.
[illegible]	[illegible]	[illegible]	[illegible]	[illegible]	[illegible]	[illegible]	[illegible]	[illegible]	[illegible]	[illegible]	[illegible]	Total of Ireland.

IRELAND.

[illegible]BLE [illegible].—QUARTER SESSIONS COURTS.—Table showing Number of Appeals from Magistrates and Applications for Spirit Licenses in the Year 18[illegible], from Returns made by Clerks of the Peace.

[illegible] COUNTY OF CITY [illegible] OF TOWN, AND PROVINCE.	Appeals from Magistrates					Applications for Spirit Licenses							
							At Annual Licensing Sessions					At other Quarter Sessions	
	Total.	[illegible]	[illegible]	Varied.	[illegible]	Total.	[illegible]	[illegible]	[illegible]	[illegible]	Otherwise disposed of.	[illegible]	[illegible]
[illegible]													
Carlow,	4	.	3	1	.	[illegible]	1	10	[illegible]	.	-	.	-
Drogheda, Town of,	-	-	-	.	.	[illegible]	1	1	.	.	1	1	.
Dublin,	[illegible]	[illegible]	.	[illegible]	1	[illegible]	7	[illegible]	6	.	4	[illegible]	13
Dublin City,	[illegible]	7	[illegible]	1	[illegible]	[illegible]	3	[illegible]	[illegible]	.	[illegible]	71	6
Kildare,	3	1	1	1	.	[illegible]	[illegible]	[illegible]	[illegible]	.	1	[illegible]	1
Kilkenny,	4	7	1	.	1	[illegible]	.	[illegible]	1	.	.	[illegible]	.
Kilkenny City,	.	.	.	.	.	[illegible]	1	[illegible]	.	.	.	[illegible]	.
King's County,	3	1	.	1	1	[illegible]	.	[illegible]	[illegible]	.	3	[illegible]	.
Longford,	.	.	.	.	.	[illegible]	.	[illegible]	1	.	[illegible]	[illegible]	[illegible]
Louth,	[illegible]	[illegible]	1	.	7	[illegible]	[illegible]	[illegible]	[illegible]	3	[illegible]	[illegible]	1
Meath,	3	[illegible]	.	.	1	[illegible]	[illegible]	[illegible]	4	.	[illegible]	[illegible]	.
Queen's County,	[illegible]	4	[illegible]	1	-	[illegible]	[illegible]	[illegible]	[illegible]	1	3	[illegible]	1
Westmeath,	4	3	.	1	-	[illegible]	[illegible]	[illegible]	4	-	4	[illegible]	[illegible]
Wexford,	[illegible]	[illegible]	4	1	7	[illegible]	[illegible]	[illegible]	[illegible]	.	[illegible]	[illegible]	[illegible]
Wicklow,	3	7	3	1	1	[illegible]	[illegible]	[illegible]	[illegible]	.	[illegible]	.	9
Total,	[illegible]	[illegible]	[illegible]	[illegible]	[illegible]	[illegible]	[illegible]	[illegible]	[illegible]	4	[illegible]	[illegible]	[illegible]
[illegible]													
Clare,	[illegible]	[illegible]	7	1	.	[illegible]	[illegible]	[illegible]	[illegible]	1	[illegible]	[illegible]	[illegible]
Cork, East Riding,	[illegible]	7	3	[illegible]	[illegible]	[illegible]	[illegible]	[illegible]	[illegible]	[illegible]	.	[illegible]	[illegible]
Cork, West Riding,	[illegible]	[illegible]	[illegible]	1	.	[illegible]	[illegible]	[illegible]	[illegible]	1	[illegible]	[illegible]	7
Cork City,	7	.	.	[illegible]	.	[illegible]	[illegible]	[illegible]	7	.	7	[illegible]	[illegible]
Kerry,	[illegible]	[illegible]	[illegible]	[illegible]	[illegible]	[illegible]	[illegible]	[illegible]	[illegible]	[illegible]	[illegible]	[illegible]	[illegible]
Limerick,	[illegible]	[illegible]	[illegible]	-	.	[illegible]	[illegible]	[illegible]	9	.	.	[illegible]	.
Limerick City,	[illegible]	.	[illegible]		-	[illegible]	[illegible]	.	.	.	.	17	[illegible]
Tipperary,	[illegible]	[illegible]	[illegible]	1	[illegible]	[illegible]	[illegible]	[illegible]	[illegible]	.	[illegible]	[illegible]	[illegible]
Waterford,	[illegible]	.	[illegible]	-	.	[illegible]	[illegible]	[illegible]	[illegible]	.	.	[illegible]	[illegible]
Waterford City,	[illegible]	.	[illegible]	-	.	[illegible]	1	[illegible]	1	.	1	[illegible]	[illegible]
Total,	[illegible]	[illegible]	[illegible]	[illegible]	[illegible]	[illegible]	[illegible]	[illegible]	[illegible]	[illegible]	[illegible]	[illegible]	[illegible]

TABLE 61.—LOCAL CHARTER COURTS.—Table of Proceedings in Lord Mayor's Court and Courts of Conscience in the Year 1898, from Returns made by the Registrars.

Names of Courts.	[illegible]	[illegible]	Number of Decrees.			Amount ordered to be paid. For Debts or Claims.	Costs.	Total Amount ordered to be paid.	No. of Warrants.	Amount of Fees in Warrants.	Amount of Fees received by Registrar.	Application of Fees. To the Treasurer.	To the Officers.	Otherwise.
						£ s. d.	£ s. d.	£ s. d.		£ s. d.	£ s. d.	£ s. d.	£ s. d.	£ s. d.
Chartered Court of Conscience,	[illegible]	[illegible]	[illegible]	-	-	[illegible]	-	[illegible]	[illegible]	[illegible]	[illegible]	-	[illegible]	[illegible]
Drogheda ditto,	[illegible]	[illegible]	[illegible]		-	[illegible]	[illegible]	[illegible]	[illegible]	[illegible]	[illegible]	-	[illegible]	-
Dublin (Lord Mayor's Court),*	-	-	-	-	-	-	-	-	-	-	-	-	-	-
Dublin Court of Conscience,	[illegible]	[illegible]	[illegible]	[illegible]	[illegible]	[illegible]	[illegible]	[illegible]	[illegible]	[illegible]	[illegible]	[illegible]	[illegible]	[illegible]
Kilkenny ditto,	[illegible]	[illegible]	[illegible]	[illegible]	-	-	-	-	[illegible]	-	-	-	-	-
Limerick ditto,	[illegible]	[illegible]	[illegible]	[illegible]	-	[illegible]	-	[illegible]	[illegible]	[illegible]	[illegible]	-	[illegible]	-
Londonderry ditto,	[illegible]	[illegible]	[illegible]	[illegible]	-	[illegible]	[illegible]	[illegible]	[illegible]	[illegible]	[illegible]	-	[illegible]	-
Wexford ditto,	[illegible]	[illegible]	[illegible]	-	-	[illegible]	-	[illegible]	[illegible]	[illegible]	[illegible]	[illegible]	[illegible]	-
Total,	[illegible]	[illegible]	[illegible]	[illegible]	[illegible]	[illegible]	[illegible]	[illegible]	[illegible]	[illegible]	[illegible]	[illegible]	[illegible]	[illegible]

TABLE 62.—IRISH LAND COMMISSION.—Return of Sales to Tenants under the Purchase of Land (Ireland) Act, 1885, in which the Loans were issued during the Years ending 31st December, 1897, and 31st December, 1898.

Provinces.	1897. Number of Tenant Purchasers.	Purchase-money agreed upon.	Amount of Loans Issued.	No. of Years' Purchase on Net Rental.	1898. No. of Tenant Purchasers.	Purchase-money agreed upon.	Amount of Loans Issued.	No. of Years' Purchase on Net Rental.
		£	£			£	£	
Ulster,	[illegible]	[illegible]	[illegible]	[illegible]	[illegible]	[illegible]	[illegible]	[illegible]
Munster,	[illegible]	[illegible]	[illegible]	[illegible]	[illegible]	[illegible]	[illegible]	[illegible]
Leinster,	[illegible]	[illegible]	[illegible]	[illegible]	[illegible]	[illegible]	[illegible]	[illegible]
Connaught,	[illegible]	[illegible]	[illegible]	[illegible]	[illegible]	[illegible]	[illegible]	[illegible]
Total,	56	[illegible]	[illegible]	[illegible]	[illegible]	[illegible]	[illegible]	[illegible]

TABLE 63.—Return of Sales to Tenants under the Purchase of Land (Ireland) Act, 1891, in which the Loans were issued during the Years ending 31st December, 1897, and 31st December, 1898.

Provinces.	1897. No. of Tenant Purchasers.	Purchase-money agreed upon.	Amount of Loans Issued.	No. of Years' Purchase on Net Rental.	1898. No. of Tenant Purchasers.	Purchase-money agreed upon.	Amount of Loans Issued.	No. of Years' Purchase on Net Rental.
		£	£			£	£	
Ulster,	[illegible]	[illegible]	[illegible]	[illegible]	[illegible]	[illegible]	[illegible]	[illegible]
Munster,	[illegible]	[illegible]	[illegible]	[illegible]	[illegible]	[illegible]	[illegible]	[illegible]
Leinster,	[illegible]	[illegible]	[illegible]	[illegible]	[illegible]	[illegible]	[illegible]	[illegible]
Connaught,	[illegible]	[illegible]	[illegible]	[illegible]	[illegible]	[illegible]	[illegible]	[illegible]
Total,	[illegible]	[illegible]	[illegible]	[illegible]	[illegible]	[illegible]	[illegible]	[illegible]

TABLE 64.—Table showing the Number of Eviction Notices filed in the High Court of Justice and County Courts in Ireland, under Section 7 of the Land Law (Ireland) Act, 1887, during the Year 1898.

—	Notices Filed.
Queen's Bench Division,	[illegible]
County Courts,	[illegible]
Total,	[illegible]

DUBLIN CASTLE,

28th April, 1900.

Sir,

I have to acknowledge the receipt of your Letter of the 26th instant, forwarding, for submission to His Excellency the Lord Lieutenant, the Judicial Statistics (Ireland), 1898, Part II.

I am, Sir,

Your obedient Servant,

J. B. DOUGHERTY.

The Registrar-General,

Charlemont House,

Rutland Square.

www.ingramcontent.com/pod-product-compliance
Lightning Source LLC
Chambersburg PA
CBHW031441270326
41930CB00007B/813